REAL-WORLD
TEEN
SERVICES

REAL-WORLD
TEEN
SERVICES

JENNIFER VELÁSQUEZ

An imprint of the American Library Association
Chicago | 2015

JENNIFER VELÁSQUEZ is a lecturer at the San José State University School of Information and coordinator of teen services for the San Antonio Public Library System. A 2011 *Library Journal* Mover & Shaker, she is the recipient of the *New York Times* Librarian Award (2005). She holds a master's degree from the Rutgers University School of Communication and Information. Jennifer consults on teen library spaces and services, and is a frequent conference speaker and professional development trainer. For the past twenty years, she has worked exclusively with teens in the public library setting.

© 2015 by the American Library Association

Extensive effort has gone into ensuring the reliability of the information in this book; however, the publisher makes no warranty, express or implied, with respect to the material contained herein.

ISBNs
978-0-8389-1342-0 (paper)
978-0-8389-1348-2 (PDF)
978-0-8389-1349-9 (ePub)
978-0-8389-1350-5 (Kindle)

Library of Congress Cataloging-in-Publication Data
Velásquez, Jennifer.
 Real-world teen services / Jennifer Velásquez.
  pages cm
 Includes bibliographical references and index.
  ISBN 978-0-8389-1342-0 (print : alk. paper) — ISBN 978-0-8389-1348-2 (pdf) — ISBN 978-0-8389-1349-9 (epub) — ISBN 978-0-8389-1350-5 (kindle)
 1. Young adults' libraries—United States. 2. Libraries and teenagers—United States. I. Title.
 Z718.5.V45 2015
 027.62'6—dc23   2015004192

Cover design by T. J. Johnson. Book composition by Dianne M. Rooney in the Charis SIL, Quicksand, and Gotham typefaces.

⊚ This paper meets the requirements of ANSI/NISO Z39.48–1992 (Permanence of Paper).

Printed in the United States of America

19 18 17 16 15   5 4 3 2 1

FOR TRAYVON

CONTENTS

Foreword, by Anthony Bernier, PhD   ix

Preface   xiii

Acknowledgments   xv

Introduction   xvii

1	TEEN LIBRARY SPACE	1
2	TEEN LIBRARY PROGRAMMING	27
3	CRAFTING SERVICE DYNAMICS AND MODELING SERVICE STRATEGIES	55
4	RULES, CONDUCT CODES, AND BEHAVIOR	69
5	ACCESS, CONTROL, AND PRIVACY	81
6	LIGHTNING ROUND: ADDRESSING COMMON ISSUES AND CONCERNS	97

Index   113

FOREWORD

I've known and admired Jennifer Velásquez since 2005, the year she "arrived" on the national scene in receiving the *New York Times* Librarian Award. I was subsequently lucky enough to recruit her to teach for us at San José State where she's since taught our introduction to YA services course. And while I know it's impolitic to say something so bold, in this case the observation is relevant: she's engineered the development of a professional YA services department at San Antonio Public Library (SAPL). She's not done it alone, of course, but it's been "Jen's" vision, professionalism, and damn hard work that's raised the profile of SAPL's YA services to national stature.

As the author of *Real-World Teen Services,* Jennifer offers new and seasoned professionals and generalists, as well as administrators, a rare combination of practice-relevant insights gained from years of successful and direct field experience, as well as a store of classroom-tested critical engagement, to provide an updated introduction to contemporary YA services.

Among the insights Jennifer draws upon from serving as an experienced panelist speaker and presenter at associational gatherings is the accurate recognition that many of the constant questions one fields as a presenter of YA services, irrespective of the topic, are questions about "the basics." The needle never seems to move much. The field never gathers sufficient momentum to move forward, and so seems forever "stuck in first gear," as I refer to it.

It is my own assessment that this circumstance is the consequence of libraries constantly thrusting librarians and other staff, for many different reasons, into YA service situations insufficiently prepared and supported. Librarians are not supported in taking additional coursework or evidence-based workshops upon assuming YA services responsibilities. They are not prepared by reading professional literature. They are not supported in making professional connections with senior practitioners or in investigating comparator institutions.

Paraprofessionals frequently find themselves left to their own devices to "cover" YA services. Consequently, when staff does get the opportunity to attend a panel or workshop facilitated by someone of Jennifer's caliber, they feel they need answers to "basic" questions.

Real-World Teen Services is thus, in part, a remedy to this lingering problem of forever being stuck in first gear.

Among the most significant interventions Jennifer offers in *Real-World Teen Services* is turning to the all-important and much ignored "why" question: Why do libraries serve young adults?

Real-World Teen Services does not recline on what so many books on YA services do in concentrating on the "what" or "how" questions . . .. Thus, this is not another book about what specific resources someone feels are important for YAs to read, although it does inform those decisions. It is not another book with "tips" about how to offer popular programs, though it informs these decisions, too.

Instead, *Real-World Teen Services* prepares the reader to argue and advocate more successfully for YA services within the institutional contexts where YA service providers all too often lose. If you can't successfully argue "why" libraries should professionally and equitably serve young adults then none of the other questions will yield satisfactory answers. And if you can't successfully argue "why" libraries should professionally and equitably serve young adults how can you expect that others will?

So, what's Jennifer's answer to this "why" question? Her answer is quite simple, really, but one libraries have historically exhibited tremendous difficulty in carrying out. Libraries, in Jennifer's formulation, ought not continue offering services filtered only through the agendas of adults—be they well-intentioned pro-youth community advocates and funders, clinical youth advocates, school officials and teachers, library administrators, or even librarians themselves. Why YA services exist is to serve young adults.

In viewing YA services from what we might call "the bottom-up," *Real-World Teen Services* thus strives to update YA services to where much of the rest of our LIS field is increasingly going—focusing on user experience rather than continuing to serve institutional assumptions, prerogatives, and priorities. One of our most respected LIS historians, Wayne Wiegand, is about to take this very same "bottom-up" approach in his comprehensive historical treatment, *"Part of Our Lives:" A People's History of the American Public Library* (forthcoming from Oxford University Press). Thus, it increasingly matters less how many titles a library counts on its shelves, how many computers it says it offers, how many library cards it issues or books it circulates, or even how many youth sign up for or attend programs.

Nor does *Real-World Teen Services* argue that it's always important to justify YA library service based on discrete "skill development" or antiquated "youth development" models freighted, as they are, with their cultural imperatives to incessantly drive youth toward some idealized "adulthood." In this new formulation libraries must offer YA services because they serve the needs and desires of young adult users right now and in the present and fleeting moment known as youth. Noted educational critic Jonathan Kozol says it best when he observed that youth "is not merely basic training for utilitarian adulthood. It should have some claims upon our mercy, not for its future value to the economic interests of competitive societies but for its present value as a perishable piece of life itself" (Kozol 2005).

Once this "why" question is addressed, as Jennifer does in *Real-World Teen Services,* the other questions can come more profitably into play for service providers, practitioners, and administrators: What are the best practices for serving YAs meanings about their library experiences? How to best deliver those services? What criteria ought libraries use to evaluate and improve them over time?

Without our institution's firm grasp on the *why* question, however, the rest of the library's YA response is, as Jennifer puts it, just "floating in uncharted waters" or, as I put it, "stuck in first gear."

Thus, more than any other recent book in YA services literature, Jennifer begins to invert the prevailing and conventional focus on the institutional or adultist agendas about "youth development," about "youth-at-risk," curriculum or skill development, or any number of ever-present moral panic discourses about young people. Instead, this book dedicates itself to focusing library work on the actual end user—user meanings, user desires, user experiences. Jennifer distills this approach into three simple words: "always trust teens."

This is not an easy thing to do in an area of library and information science so dramatically lacking in grounded research as YA services. It is not an easy thing to face down historically driven adult agendas that envision libraries as a means to "improve" young people, to help "keep them off the streets," or help them "become adults." It's especially difficult to push back on these imposed agendas when the field languishes in first gear, without evidence, about what even constitutes best practices; a field always needing to ask questions about "the basics."

Ultimately this book argues that you're not really "welcoming" people into a service if all of the experiences and meanings have been predetermined by someone else.

On the other hand, without asking such an important question as "why," YA service providers will never be able to get into second gear to drive the work forward.

So, read *Real-World Teen Services* to gain this important perspective on current YA services as it applies directly to some "basic" practices such as YA spaces, programming, staffing, and the implications of library rules. Then see for yourself how this increasingly potent focus on the end-user can get your own view of YA services out of first and into second gear.

Anthony Bernier, PhD

Associate Professor, San José State University, iSchool

Editor, *Transforming Young Adult Services*

Oakland, California

January 2015

REFERENCE

Kozol, Jonathan. 2005. "Still Separate, Still Unequal: America's Educational Apartheid." *Harper's Magazine* 311 (September 1).

PREFACE

A few years ago, I did a presentation at the ALA Annual Conference about teens' mobile technology usage patterns and their implications for libraries. It was specific, and—I believed—thought-provoking stuff. When the allotted question period arrived, librarians from around the country began to ask basic questions about basic teen library services and situations. It wasn't the first time that the topic at hand was pushed aside by a hunger to talk about "the basics."

When I began my journey as a teen services librarian in the late 1990s, I was in seemingly uncharted waters. My first task was to cobble together "teen services" out of good intentions and dust.

I found few resources beyond lists of YA fiction books and litanies of "cool" teen programming ideas. By trial, error (read: epic failures), and instinct, things came together. Some twenty years later, I'm left with one unshakable belief about teen library services: always trust teens. Always. Relevance and success mean being truly open to teens' ideas and desires about their library experience. It's not that your ideas are bad—they are just *your* ideas and this isn't about you or your ideas or what you think a library should be. This is about teens—as partners, producers, and participants.

In this book, I've endeavored to use real-world examples to address the challenges universally faced by teen services library people. The use of the term *real-world* in the book's title acknowledges the need for better calibration of library practitioners' expectations regarding teen services. It is also a call to reframe the established service hierarchy from one that depends on adult mediation to one that relies on activation of library services by the teen end user.

My inspiration came from questions I've consistently received over the years from teen services people and the students in my introduction to YA services course at San José State University's iSchool. I try to address those questions—and to pose some new ones. The book encourages practitioners and LIS students to place an understanding of the teen end user first among the characteristics of a successful teen services professional. It is vital that teen services professionals support each other to reach this crucial shift in service attitude. To encourage this, in the final chapter of this book you will hear the unique service perspectives of two of my former students, as well as a former colleague at the San Antonio Public Library System.

Serving as both a practitioner and an academic has allowed me to view teen services with two sets of eyes: as a librarian/manager/administrator involved in the day-to-day operations of teen services in a large urban library setting, and as an academic who examines teen services issues, asks questions, identifies patterns and problems, and seeks solutions.

I hope you find this book helpful and that it frames fresh ways of thinking about teens, libraries, and our role as teen services librarians—the lone wolves, the magicians tasked with producing miracles out of good intentions and dust.

I hope to hear from you so that this conversation may continue.

Jennifer Velásquez
@jenVLSQZ

ACKNOWLEDGMENTS

Deepest thanks to colleagues, muses, mentors, and devil's advocates:

Viki Ash, Helayne Beavers, Anthony Bernier, Martin Brynskov, Lotte duwe Nielsen, Dan Freeman, June Garcia, Angela Gwizdala, Rolf Hapel, Henrik Jochumsen, Lisbeth Mærkedahl, Marie Østergaard, Louise Overgaard, Ramiro Salazar, Jamie Santoro, Roberta Sparks, and Stephanie Zvirin; my colleagues at Aarhus Kommunes Biblioteker/DOKK1, San Antonio Public Library, and San José State University iSchool; and the entire staff of ALA Editions.

Love and gratitude to family and friends:

Gabriel, Barbara, Joseph, Ofelia, Willie, Carol, Robert, Gianna, Sophia, Edmund, Bianca, Adam, Judith, Guillermo, Citlali, Cynthia, Marie, and Cimi.

INTRODUCTION

Contradictions and Complexity
Twenty-First-Century Teens in a Nineteenth-Century Library

The traditional structure of the library is at odds with the ways teens want to use public space: discover, share, and create information and interact with their peers, community, and adults.

Habitually perpetuating and imposing the conventions of the nineteenth-century library on twenty-first-century teens is a prescription for failure. Teens, whose intentions with information are at once traditional, complex, and completely new, come to the library with a unique set of expectations. A library's rules, policies, spaces, atmosphere, and procedures can undermine the possibilities the library has to offer.

The Public Library Data Services Report (www.ala.org/pla/publica tions/plds) publishes the results of the Public Library Association's survey of North American libraries. This data reveals that full-time staffing for teens has decreased just as many libraries are moving forward with high-profile initiatives targeted to teen users (YALSA 2013). Many teen services librarians function alone in their organization, and can experience isolation because of organizational structure or the often low social status of their service group.

Teen services librarians often need to explain who they are, what they do, and what the library has to offer to this audience. The purpose of this book is to help current and future teen services librarians grasp the *why,* even as they work in a service landscape that focuses on *what* and *how.*

A recurring theme in the book is instinct versus articulation. Although teen services people may know and understand issues on an instinctive level, they must be prepared to articulate these ideas in the face of threats to teen service.

This book begins with an examination of the physical space libraries dedicate to teens. The first chapter deals with how to make the most of the limited square footage available in many libraries. It deals with concepts of the physical space of the library as it relates to teens by presenting big picture space models that can be scaled to fit large or small teen spaces. Included is a look at the meaning of space in public buildings and the manner in which libraries rely on imitation rather than research in the development of spaces for teens. It contains a brief examination of participatory culture theory and affinity space and includes an examination of the Danish Four-Space Model.

Chapter 1 also looks at common pitfalls that occur when activating a teen library space and suggests remedies. It reviews the reasons to make these spaces "teens only," and discusses common concerns such as restrictions and staffing. The chapter explains why teen participation is the ideal driver for the development of teen space. It concludes with a real-world section offering strategies for beginning the process of claiming teen space using the shelving of the YA collection.

Chapter 2 looks at programming for teens and asks why teens often don't attend these library programs. The teen services librarian needs to articulate how teen programming fits into broader library and teen services contexts. The chapter discusses common organizational barriers to teen programming, including the library's physical layout and resistance from colleagues and administration. It urges teen services librarians to examine how their own expectations and preconceptions may be a barrier to effective teen programming.

Suggestions to help teen services librarians move from an inward-facing siloed process to one that shifts the librarians' roles from creators to facilitators of teen participation in the development and implementation of teen programming for themselves and their peers. The chapter proposes a number of forms that teen programming can take.

Chapter 3 illustrates why it is vital for teen services librarians to help all members of library staff learn how to serve teens effectively, and why crafting a positive image of teen services in the organization is paramount. The chapter proposes methods whereby teen services librarians can model outstanding teen service strategies for colleagues, and describes how to create a readers' advisory strategy that does not fetishize the book or author. It also suggests that organizations intentionally staff for service to teens rather than rely on serendipity of staff interests related to teen services.

Chapter 4 focuses on the development and application of rules by library staff, and overviews strategies for managing problem behavior from both teens and staff members. It offers suggestions for advocacy when formulating and applying library rules, discusses the inherent problems that occur when there are separate sets of rules for different populations or library spaces, and describes how the rules are best communicated to teen patrons. The chapter ends with suggestions about when to involve authorities and about the importance of maintaining a professional tone in even the most trying situations.

In contrast to chapter 4's discussion of how a library articulates behavioral expectations (i.e., how the library expects users to act), chapter 5 deals with the access and control issues that a library's policies and procedures imposes on patrons (i.e., how the library treats its users), and the implications these limitations may have on teen patron privacy. The chapter treats the subjects of truancy, restrictions on when teens can use the library and what activities are allowed, and situations that may arise when teens volunteer information about serious personal situations to library staff.

In chapter 6, the book closes with a question-and-answer section that considers common but often overlooked teen services issues, and includes responses from practicing teen services professionals. Topics range from "What do you do when teen patrons want to say hello by hugging you?" to "What are some strategies for effective teen services when you are the only teen services librarian in the library system tasked with serving all the teens?"

The primary audience for this book is teen services librarians and library science students studying teen services. Generalists who wish to gain some insight into teen services can use it and, for administrators in particular, it offers a tableau of the real-world challenges that may be invisible to management in the library setting.

The book describes real-world tactics that can be applied in a variety of service situations, and addresses a variety of challenges and threats to teen services. Each chapter closes with a Soap Box Moment that offers unfiltered advice for practitioners or food for thought for future teen services librarians.

The goal of this book is to address issues and challenges that are seldom discussed in the professional literature; to offer practical advice, strategies, and tactics grounded in experience and best practices that will improve service to teens; and to reframe and advance the way teen services librarians and their colleagues approach teen end users and teen library services.

REFERENCE

Young Adult Library Services Association. 2013. Board of Directors Meeting Minutes. ALA Midwinter Meeting, January 25 – 29. www.ala.org/yalsa/sites/ala.org.yalsa/files/content/Administrators_MW13.pdf.

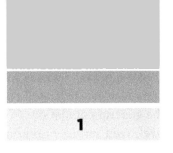

1

TEEN LIBRARY SPACE

KEY CONSIDERATIONS

- How does the library space foster opportunities for authentic teen participation and ownership of the library experience?
- How and to what degree can teens control and shape their physical environment in the library?
- How can teen participation be ongoing and sustainable, and how can physical space foster this process?
- How can physical space be adjusted to accommodate the evolving interests and activities teens want to engage in?

A Dedicated Teen Space

Cultivating a space in the library that teens can activate and own sends teens a strong signal they are valued and welcome in the library. Making the case to managers for a dedicated teen space may be challenging, particularly in library locations where space is at a premium, the idea of teens congregating is problematic, or competition for resources is fierce.

Teens (defined here as those ages thirteen to eighteen) are usually scrutinized closely because of expectations that they will cause trouble. They are often held to different behavioral expectations than other patrons—a group of toddlers or genealogists will be greeted with smiles and nods, but a group of exuberant teens is likely to get thrown out. This may cause managers to view dedicated teen space as a means to segregate teens from the general population.

On an instinctive level, teen services librarians may know that it is important to provide teens with dedicated space in the library. As their advocates, teen services librarians must be able to:

- articulate why a dedicated teen space is important
- make a case for teen space to managers, coworkers, and community members
- express how space is a link to effective and efficient services, programming, and overall service equality

The form this message takes is crucial. Managers may be more receptive to an established, documented rationale from outside of the organization. Such a rationale may provide weight to a space request/justification for teens.

In addition to offering a rationale for teen space, examining proven space models—even if they are not related specifically to teen space—may offer teen services librarians fresh perspectives and reveal new possibilities for the use of space to fulfill overall service goals for teens. This can also help to change the habitual, imitative patterns of teen space development perpetuated in current practice.

Teen services librarians should not focus on the physical features of a teen space, but rather on the service reasons behind why the library should offer dedicated space to teens. They should consider how teen space is developed; how library space models can be applied to craft space for teen users; and what their implications are for teen services.

The Meaning of Space

Space is power. The allotment of space in public buildings clearly illustrates which groups matter and which groups don't. In Anthony Bernier's groundbreaking research on teen library spaces, he notes that although many library systems recognize the need for dedicated space for teens, there is very little research on YA spaces in public libraries, despite growing interest in the topic over the last dozen years (Bernier 2013). Attention has focused on how teen spaces look and the features they include. However, without adequate grounding in research, the construction of new spaces and remodels of existing spaces often do not take into account the unique needs of teens, the way they desire to use and naturally use space.

Because there is so little research, architects, designers, and librarians often select design elements for teen spaces without any basis in best practices. This reliance on untested models can result in design echo chambers where libraries copy features from each other without considering functionality or the specific needs and behaviors of the user group. The resulting spaces are often stages for conflict, which place teens engaging in normal usage behavior in environments that simply don't work for their normal—and appropriate—needs or habits. Bernier describes this phenomenon as the "Geography of No!," where libraries enforce regulations and create spaces that force teens into behaviors and environments that directly contradict how young people actually work and use space (Bernier 2003).

Designing teen spaces isn't about tables, chairs, and trendy lounge seating; it's about intention and usefulness. Because there are no best practices, practitioners must rely on common practice. If there is no clear vision for the space beyond warehousing YA fiction or equipment labs without context, the result may be teen library space that is not sufficiently welcoming, or which discourages engagement, participation, and teen ownership. The resulting ambiguity can manifest as:

- a lack of focus on what will happen in the space
- rigid and limiting ideas about how the space will be used
- an off-target age-range of clientele (older children versus teens versus adults)
- a space that forces user behavior that does not accommodate the activities teens engage in naturally
- a reliance upon features rather than responsive service and staffing models that cultivate experience
- a subtext of using space to control the clientele group

Form Follows Function

The American architect Louis Sullivan coined the phrase "form (ever) follows function" in 1896. Sullivan is noted for developing the shape of the steel skyscraper in the late nineteenth century, a time when shifts in technology, taste, and economic forces precipitated the abandonment of established architectural styles. Architectural critics of the time proposed that this new type of building, which was multi-story and included the newly developed elevator, should incorporate classical forms, and that traditional style elements and patterns should be applied to its design. This aesthetic is reflected in Chicago's tall office buildings, which are frosted with classical columns and dressed as gothic cathedrals. Sullivan suggested that this new type of building needed an honest style that what this building looked like and its form should not be informed by the past but be determined by its function (Sullivan 1896).

An examination of the form of the public library building illustrates the same notion of applied traditional forms. Although what libraries offer users—the functions of technology, services, resources, programming, and gathering spaces—has evolved rapidly over the past few decades, the physical form of the library building has, for the most part, stayed constant.

THE CARNEGIE MODEL

The traditional public library building also has a classical precedent. During the late nineteenth and early twentieth centuries, industrialist Andrew Carnegie funded the construction of thousands of public libraries. The Carnegie Model divided library space into two wings—one for children and one for adults. The adult wing provided functional space for work and to warehouse books. The children's wing provided functional space where adults helped children mediate the notions of reading, language, and books. Teens seemingly did not exist in a building model with one wing for children and one wing for adults "with YAs neglected as neither or both" (Bernier 2013).

The different areas of the library can be defined by function (circulation, reference, access to technology), or by service population (children, teens, and adults). The children's section is generally the most easily recognizable part of a library because the clientele is usually of a particular physical stature, the material is visually distinct, and the hallmark service for children—the traditional story time—comes with a set of established and recognizable spatial needs and manifestations. The children's space in a library is not necessarily meant to be used independently by children, but also by parents and caregivers who mediate the experience of the space for them, and who most likely initiated the visit to the library space. Teens, however, engage in many activities independently (i.e., without mediation of a parent or staff).

Because teen services is a new tradition, there is little scholarship and few best practices that address space planning. The following section reviews relevant theory and practices.

Teen Participation in the Development of Space

A cornerstone of teen library services is the principle that teens must be actively involved in decisions about their library experience. YALSA's *Teen Space Guidelines* suggest that teens be included in planning and be given decision-making roles in the development of space intended for their use. The active participation of teens ensures that their evolving needs and interests are being addressed, and that they will play a key role in attracting peers to the library (YALSA 2012).

Teens who are enthusiastically engaged in planning and decision-making are likely to develop a sense of ownership of the library that will enhance the quality of their library experience. This begins with the space intended for teens in the library.

YALSA guidelines for the development of teen library space suggest libraries should:

- Create a space that meets the needs of teens in the community by asking teens to play a role in the planning process
- Solicit teen feedback in the design of the space and regarding its use to allow teens to develop a sense of ownership
- Solicit teen feedback in the development of policies to ensure the space is representative of teen needs (YALSA 2012)

When libraries involved teens in planning new teen spaces, higher levels of youth participation correlated to a range of positive outcomes in the design and execution of new and renovated library teen spaces. These positive outcomes include staff satisfaction, service quality, larger teen spaces, increased funding opportunities, decreased concern with behavioral problems, and greater sensitivity to green options and sustainability in building materials (Bernier, Males, and Rickman 2014).

Encouraging and cultivating teen participation in the space-development process begins by involving teens in focus groups and asking them what they want. But how can teen participation be continuously fostered by physical space?

It is valuable to examine the tenets of participatory culture theory to gain an understanding of large- and small-scale applications of teen participation in space development. In *Confronting the Challenges of Participatory Culture,* Jenkins et al. (2006) describe a participatory culture as one:

- With relatively low barriers to artistic expression and civic engagement
- With strong support for creating and sharing one's creations with others
- With some type of informal mentorship whereby what is known by the most experienced is passed along to novices
- Where members believe that their contributions matter
- Where members feel some degree of social connection with one another (at the least they care what other people think about what they have created)

One of the tenets of a participatory culture is that not every member must contribute, but all members must believe they are free to contribute, and that what they contribute will be appropriately valued. Library space can foster this. Providing a participatory space for teens offers them a tangible venue to begin to take ownership of the library—teens can plant their flags and mark territory within the public space—and to customize it in a way that is different from other public venue experiences and opportunities, and is uniquely theirs. Ultimately, it allows teens to achieve a more empowered conception of citizenship (Jenkins et al. 2006).

Although teens are allowed to use public spaces like city parks, they are generally not allowed to direct its design, decoration, use, or ultimately determine how the space is experienced. A teen library space can be a public space developed in partnership with the intended users. This ownership is sustained through continuous reinforcement.

EXAMPLE: THE ANALOG DISPLAY WALL

In recent years, the idea of teen participation has primarily been associated with the use of technology and Web 2.0, but this participation can manifest through low-tech, low-cost means. Something many libraries may already be doing is displaying teen-created art in a teen space. Examining this practice through the lens of user participation can help teen librarians understand and apply a participatory context to such activities.

An analog display wall is a relatively low-tech method that encourages teen participation. It is a wall in a teen space where any teens can display their artwork. There are supplies readily available for teens to create drawings—teens can choose to draw and then to display their artwork on the wall.

This type of display differs from a wall where only sanctioned or adult-selected art is permanently installed, or one on which a group of teens have created a mural, which becomes static once completed, and may give any teens who were not involved in the project a sense that they are visiting someone else's space.

If teens are constantly creating and changing what is on the wall, will it look as an adult would like it to look? Probably not. But it will always reflect the users' tastes, interests, and desires. This isn't about adult aesthetics, but about teen participation. When libraries set up teen spaces that look too perfect or pristine, they eliminate possible avenues for teens to explore, create, and participate in immediate, spontaneous, and unexpected ways.

Big Picture Space Models

AFFINITY SPACE

The idea of the affinity space comes from the concept of participatory culture. An affinity space is "a place or set of places where people affiliate with others based primarily on shared activities, interests, and goals" (Gee 2004). The library can function as an affinity space where formal and informal activities are based on the interests teens bring to the library. These formal and informal activities occur in a peer-to-peer manner, with teens functioning as innovators and experts in their areas of interest, and library staff functioning in the role of facilitators.

Suggested in the concept of affinity space is a shift in the notion of the use of library space from a space that warehouses resources (as in the

Carnegie Model), to a space for producing social experiences and incorporating user meanings (Ito et al. 2010; London et al. 2010). Libraries that cultivate an affinity space for teens create a venue focusing on the relationships teens have with information and one another, and the creation of content, artifacts, and knowledge.

Teen services librarians should look at library spaces for teens in a new way. In many ways, the teen services portion of the physical library is first to manifest changes in service delivery models and advances in public-facing technology for a given clientele group (as in Charlotte Mecklenburg Library's ImaginOn [http://imaginon.org/default.asp] and Chicago Public Library's YouMedia [http://youmediachicago.org]). These groundbreaking spaces anticipated the shift in use of library spaces/ functions that are only now beginning to manifest in adult/family/ all-ages space in the form of content creation labs and so-called maker-spaces and Fab Labs.

What teen services should strive for is not a Fab Lab, but a Fab Library. The key to a successful library teen space is not features, but experiences. This shift in the physical space offered to teens mirrors the way teens naturally use space. The affinity space should accommodate and foster activities that teens automatically engage in like socializing, working together in groups sharing ideas/resources/content, group play, peer mentorship, and creating things like artwork or digital content. The teen space is a place where teens bring their interest to explore, rather than having sanctioned interests imposed upon them.

During this developmental stage, when teens desire to become both strong individuals and be part of a group, they naturally self-identify by interest. In social settings, teens seek to share their interests and discover those of other teens. When teens who share mutual interests gather in the library the anatomy of what can occur in the space is shaped. The experience of the space encourages the celebration of and engagement in a given interest, activity, or topic. This can occur in an ad hoc manner that is clunky and uncomfortable, or seemingly flawless by merit of a flexible neutral space, and—most importantly—appropriate staff interaction/activation that facilitates and harnesses the robust possibilities presented by the scenario. Libraries recognizing and seeking to use this energy/activity to better meet the unique needs of teens engage in the conscious shifting of traditional library space toward affinity space.

The library becomes a blank slate to which teens bring their established interests and come together around these interests, delving in to the level they wish, from passing fancy to expertise. In this the library is neutral. Then the space must yield itself to the interests and desired activities of teens.

This affinity space creates avenues to teen participation in the development and implementation of teen programming for themselves and their peers. In this way, the physical space helps in the development of teen programming and activities.

THE NORDIC LIBRARY OF THE FUTURE:
THE FOUR-SPACE MODEL FOR PUBLIC LIBRARIES

In contrast to the Carnegie Model is the Nordic Library of the Future, the four-space model. This elegant and thorough model of public library

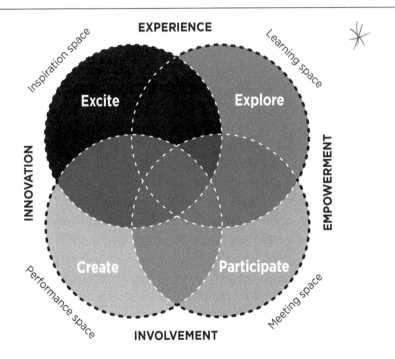

Figure 1.1   Danish Four-Space Model

Adapted from "A New Model for the Public Library in the Knowledge and Experience Society," © Dorte Skot-Hansen, Casper Huenfgaaro Rasmussen, Henrik Jochumsen.

space has at its heart the notion of participation and a set of concrete possibilities that the new library must offer users to experience, discover, participate, and create in the library context.

Developed in 2010 by Denmark's Committee on Public Libraries in the Knowledge Society, the four-space model has been used for the development of libraries in different ways, ranging from major expansion programs to minor changes in the arrangement of library branches (Danish Agency for Library and Media 2010; hereafter referenced as DALM 2010). Although the model is not specific to teen library spaces, its overarching principles can be successfully applied to teen library spaces or elements of teen services spaces.

According to the model, the library's overall objective is to support the following four possibilities for users:

- Experience
- Involvement
- Empowerment
- Innovation (DALM 2010)

The four-space model translates these possibilities into a framework consisting of four different but overlapping physical spaces: learning space, meeting space, performance space, and inspiration space. The model is useful for implementation as well as analysis. The four distinct, yet overlapping, spaces that it describes relate to service goals and respond to the behaviors and activities teens engage in within the library setting. Although the interests of teens will vary based on community, culture, era, economics, trends, and other factors, the manner in which teens use space and the library's goals are more universal.

The four-space model can be a useful tool for assessing, developing, building, arranging, and rearranging teen library spaces. It suggests that the library as a whole must offer teen users opportunities to experience, discover, participate, and create. Teen services is uniquely positioned to form teen services spaces around the four possibilities. Note that none of these physical spaces (or the activities or outcomes associated with them) is more important than the others.

LEARNING SPACE: From Reading Room to Flexible Learning Space

The idealized image of teens learning in the library is of quiet "students" individually toiling away on homework after school. Any teen services librarian knows that the after-school rush is rarely quiet, and that teens prefer to work together on projects and use a variety of resource formats. They seamlessly multitask, mixing social, recreational, and assignment-related activities. Learning activities aren't necessarily related to school, but may be based on interests teens have developed from their life situations, or may be purely recreational. The library is the ideal venue for teens to engage in all these types of learning based on all of these interests.

The four-space model can help teen services librarians conceptualize the forms learning can take, in the library setting.

- Learning can be driven by the interests of teens with their peers serving as experts or mentors.
- Learning can be analog or digital, structured or unstructured.
- Learning can take place in informal settings that may not have been designed specifically for it.
- Learning may not resemble what goes on in school, or take place in silence.

LEARNING SPACE: Implications for Teen Services

The library's classical learning space in the pre-digital age was the reading room. It was quiet and provided access to reference material (DALM 2010). In the digital age more flexible spaces are needed to meet the changing expectations of teens. This flexible space recognizes evolving learning styles, accommodates a variety of information creation and delivery mechanisms, and fosters opportunities to develop extracurricular, interest-based participatory learning. A learning space for teens should be open, inviting, nonexclusive, and accommodate different learning situations. As with the other spaces in the four-space model, the learning space can stand alone as a separate space or as an overlay of the general teen space.

■ ■ ■

MEETING SPACE: From Empty Space to Active Space

Libraries traditionally include a meeting room that is used for a variety of activities, from story time to voting. The meeting room is generally the venue where library programming, presentations, community meetings, and other activities take place.

Generally, competition for use of the meeting room is high, with community groups vying for use along with library programing requirements. However, when no activities are scheduled, the meeting room—which can often represent a sizable spatial investment—is just a big (locked) empty space.

In the four-space model, the word *meeting* transcends the idea of a formal gathering with a stated purpose and includes the idea of any social gathering. Teens enthusiastically seek out and participate in social gatherings, but there are few public meeting spaces where they can get together. However, when teens congregate in groups, it may look as though they are just loitering. A meeting space where teens can gather is a valuable community asset, even if it is only an area with tables or other seating arrangements. The space can take the form a lounge or café, or be a room that can be used for organized or spontaneous meetings.

The library is the ideal venue for teens to gather and socialize. Teen services librarians can rethink how meeting spaces can function in the library, recognizing it as:

- a "third space" between home and school
- a place to meet new people
- a neutral space where teens from a variety of socioeconomic and ethnic backgrounds can interact
- a space that fosters both formal or spontaneous discussions

MEETING SPACE: Implications for Teen Services

It isn't necessary to dedicate a separate meeting room for teen activities. Consider the possibilities if the functions of a meeting room were superimposed on the main body of the teen space—if teen meetings and programming took place within the teen space itself. There are benefits to using the designated teen space for these activities instead of scheduling them in traditional meeting rooms. Conducting formal meetings in the same space that teens use for smaller-scale or spontaneous activities reinforces teen ownership of that space and the age-specific collection housed there.

This also has positive side effects. It eliminates competition for traditional meeting rooms. And, when teen activities take place in the open, it showcases those activities and welcomes teens to join in. Visibility is important. Both library staff and the public learn about what teens do in the library. Adults are more likely to develop positive feelings toward these activities when they are demystified and promoted by occurring in the open on the service floor.

■ ■ ■

PERFORMANCE SPACE: From Stage to Screen

The four-space model closely links performance space (i.e., what is traditionally provided as a stage for events) with the idea that the library is a place for making things. The model calls this concept the *creation library*. The creation library expands the library's traditional role. It becomes a place where media conveying information, knowledge, art, and entertainment is created (DALM 2010). It becomes a library that houses a range of equipment and facilities to help authors, editors, performers, and other creators to prepare new work—alone or in groups, in new or old media, for personal use or widespread distribution (Levien 2011).

So, rather than thinking of these performances as scheduled programs presented by experts (e.g., where a pianist from the symphony does a "program"), the performance space in the four-space model implies that the library is a place for the creation of the work/product/artifact/content *as well as* a venue for performance, display, and dissemination.

This gives the teen services librarian the opportunity to rethink the teen space as a means to foster creativity and creation, where:

- teen performers can be seen by an audience—it provides opportunities that allow for spontaneous or planned performance
- teens' creative work, including artwork and writing, can be displayed and disseminated
- teens can practice and create audio, video, text, visual art, and digital content
- creation and cocreation are driven by the interests and needs of teens

PERFORMANCE SPACE: Implications for Teen Services

Teen services has been part of maker culture for decades, providing access to tools that support creative expression (both analog and digital), and supporting the creation of products through peer-to-peer and mentor assistants. The performance space reinforces the shift in teen services, from teens solely being consumers of information to becoming creators of information and content. The four-space model seeks to formalize the use of space for creating, disseminating, and showcasing user-created content and artifacts. The traditional craft table, the video editing station, and the 3-D printer (and whatever tools that will come out of future technology) serve the same purpose to the same end for this target age-group.

■ ■ ■

INSPIRATION SPACE: From Transaction to Experiences
Inspiration space encompasses the experience created for the user in the library setting. It is about how the elements encountered while visiting the library affect the user—in other words, how the library makes teens feel. To this end, the four-space model posed a critical question, "Why not choose the bookshop if it offers an altogether more cool experience?" (Hvenegaard Rasmussen, Jochumsen, and Skot-Hansen 2008). Why, indeed?

An inspiration space speaks to the ways libraries can employ elements of the *experience economy* used in retail to engage users. Any business that wants to survive in a competitive market can no longer succeed by just offering goods and services; instead, it must actively engineer new experiences, and each of its products or services must tell a story that will leave distinct emotional tracks (Pine and Gilmore 1999). Transactions are useful, service is helpful, but experience is memorable—and potentially transformative (Forrest 2009).

Because the inspiration space is perhaps the subtlest of the spaces recommended in the four-space model, it warrants a concrete example. California's Cerritos Library pioneered the application of the experience economy concept in the public library setting. Because the library is located near both Disneyland and Knott's Berry Farm, these entertainment giants offered context and inspiration for the Cerritos Library's design and, by extension, services.

City Librarian Don Buckley explains it this way: "The question isn't 'Did you find a book to read?' The question is 'How did you feel about your trip to the library?'" (Buckley 2013). As the four-space model suggests, at a time when titles and information are accessible via different virtual platforms, it is less important to ensure that visitors find what they need, and more important to help them discover what they did not know they need (DALM 2010).

For Buckley, the Cerritos Library isn't an "in-and-out library"—a place where people enter, check out materials, and leave. It is a place where they go to spend time. The goal is to make the library a destination. It's about getting to people's feelings—not just their brains—their hearts (Buckley 2013).

The possibilities inherent in the inspiration space give teen services librarians the opportunity to rethink the teen space as it relates to experiences. They should consider:

- the customer service experience teens have while interacting with staff
- the arrangement of desks and seating
- the aesthetics of the space—is it age appropriate for teens? (as opposed to older children or tweens)
- ways to encourage serendipity and surprises to make room for the unexpected so that users find inspiration for new experiences (Bjørneborn 2008)

INSPIRATION SPACE: Implications for Teen Services

Libraries have the opportunity to provide transformative experiences for teens. Granted, not every library can boast a life-sized Tyrannosaurus Rex skeleton and a 15,000 gallon aquarium (like the Cerritos Library). But every teen services librarian can step back and assess the experience imposed by the location's teen space.

Although the four-space model is aspirational, teen services librarians can strive to create a variety of experiential possibilities. They must understand that if form truly follows function, libraries must offer teen spaces that foster flexibility and responsiveness to changes, whether permanently or for a single afternoon.

Not every element of the guidelines need be adopted by every public library, but the guidelines can be a place to begin the conversation about what constitutes excellent library space for teens.

There is certainly a great deal of overlap in the four-space model—this is part of its genius. If librarians can think of the library's teen space as all of these things at the same time, they will be more likely to recognize the nexus between form and function and expand their concept of what is possible in the library space when teens can gather, learn, lead, and own their space.

Regardless of whether they have many or few resources, teen services librarians should not be complacent about how physical space affects the experience the library offers teens. Familiarity with a space makes it easy to overlook its defects. Examining how teens are inclined to use space, and reassessing how space is allocated in the library—taking a fresh view of even the smallest space in the context of big picture space models— can help make the teen library experience richer and more inviting.

Teens-Only Space

Teen services librarians may find that an existing teen space does not function well because it is not reserved for use by its intended clientele. Ideally, teen services space should be dedicated for use by teens (thirteen to eighteen years of age) only.

Teen services librarians may experience resistance when proposing that the library provide a space that is "teens only," or that it change policy to reserve an existing teen space exclusively for teens only. The desire to avoid confrontation may lead libraries to not designate a space "teens only" because they don't want to have the inevitable conversations about why the library provides a space for this target age group.

The Young Adult Library Services Association (YALSA) has developed guidelines for creating teen space. Although not grounded in research, the guidelines are a good starting point that can begin a discussion about, and evaluation of, a public library's success in providing physical space dedicated to teens (YALSA 2012).

YALSA's space guidelines describe the benefits of reserving a space where teens are the primary occupants and where they are buffered from threatening adult-initiated interactions. Use of the teen-only space should be limited to adults browsing materials for a controlled period of time not to exceed fifteen minutes, tutors currently working with teen students, and library staff. Or a teen library space can allow adults to access the YA collection housed in a teen space. The posted rules of the Teen Central area of Phoenix's Burton Barr Library state that adults may use the collection, but they may not hang out.

Although YALSA guidelines suggest that adults accompanied by a teen should be allowed in the area, this suggestion is problematic. The presence of parents, for example, can significantly change the dynamic of the space. Parents should be advised that the area is for teens only, but they are welcome to drop in periodically to check on their teenaged children.

Beyond what is suggested by YALSA, a teens-only area sends the message that the library values teens by reserving a space in the library where they can take ownership. The library can further cultivate teen participation if they develop the space and allow it to evolve.

COLONIZATION BY ADULTS AND IMPERIALIZATION BY CHILDREN

If a library's teen space is desirable and well-appointed, or even if it is not, adults may feel entitled to use it or have their children use it. Older children ages nine to twelve who self-identify as teens will think the teen space is intended for their use.

When teens enter the library they should be able to find the space reserved for them—perhaps this is indicated by a sign or another visual cue. However, if that space is occupied by adults or children, then it isn't really a teen space. If the designated space is occupied, teens may choose to congregate in another area of the building or to leave the library entirely, and they might not ever return. This should not be construed as teens choosing not to use their space in the library, because the library has in fact *not* provided a space for them. If the space belongs to everyone, it belongs to no one.

SCHEDULED TEENS-ONLY TIMES

The realities of square footage keep many libraries from reserving an area solely for use by teen patrons. The solution to offering a teen space might be to allow adults and children to use the teen space for a portion of the day. This way, during the times when teens are in school the area can be used for other purposes. This might be a solution for small library locations where the teen space is carved out of a general space—allow for general public use of the space during school hours and create signage and policy that define teens-only times in the space (usually after-school hours and weekends during the school year and most days during the summer).

This solution works only if staff manages the transition from "everyone's space" to teens-only space at the designated time. A designated teens-only schedule will not succeed if there are no procedures in place, or existing rules are not enforced to ensure that adults or children aren't occupying the area during the time periods reserved for teens only. If teens arrive and the space is filled with adults and children they will be unlikely to use the space.

Staff must take a proactive role in clearing out the teen space at designated times, even if there are no teens in the building. Allow thirty minutes between the time adults and children are asked to leave the area and the after-school rush hour. Regular adult patrons (including parents) will soon learn the schedule, eliminating awkward "the teens are here now and you have to leave" moments.

Staff must enforce this procedure and understand it is not optional. Teen services staff should teach their colleagues in the best way to manage this transition. To ensure that all staff members are on the same page, the teen services librarian should explain the rationale for and importance of a teens-only space and offer suggestions about what to say to patrons when asking them to vacate the space. For example, if the space becomes teens-only at 4:30 pm, staff should begin warning adult patrons at 3:30 pm every day. Sample dialogue might include:

> Sir, just to let you know, in about 30 minutes, this space will become a teens-only area. I'll be glad to help you find another space in the library that you can occupy after 4 pm.

> Ma'am, after 4 pm, this space is reserved for teens 13 to 18 only. So, that's in about 15 minutes. I'll be glad to help you find another place to sit with your child.

Table tents that warn adults and parents that the space is reserved for teens during certain hours will inform users and reinforce the message that staff deliver verbally. The signs must be reprinted as needed and steps should be taken to keep them looking fresh. However, these fair-warning table signs are not a substitute for staff's in-person notification.

Pitfalls and Bad Habits

TEEN SPACE—NOT TWEEN SPACE

Older children ages nine through twelve (sometimes called *tweens*) are aspirational teens, and they often want to emulate teen culture and engage in teen activities. Although older children may not feel at home in the children's area, allowing them to congregate in the teen area is a disservice to the teens for whom the space is intended. A sign that reads "teens" or "teens only" may serve to attract older children and indicate to them and their parents that the space may be intended for their use.

If older children are permitted to congregate in the designated teen space, the library has, in effect, developed *two* children's spaces: one for younger children and one for older children—with teens being marginalized.

Just as teens will avoid a designated teens-only space if it is filled with adults, they will not use the space if it is filled with older children. This avoidance behavior may result in librarians assuming that teen users neither want nor need a designated library space. This assumption may result in a decision to allow older children to use the teen space. The teen services librarian may hear the manager say something like, "We've provided a space for teens but 'they' don't ever use it, but the tweens do." Because older children visualize themselves as teens they're eager to use the teen space, and will colonize a teen space just as adults will, if given the chance.

The same steps used to keep adults out of a teen space should be employed by staff to keep the space free of older children. Inform older children and their parents that the area is a teens-only space and kindly but firmly ask them to respect that the space is reserved for teens. Remind them that when they turn thirteen the space will be theirs.

Teens often come to the library by themselves, but older children are generally *taken* to the library by adults who can be vocal advocates. Parents may insist that their children be allowed to use a teen space. When this occurs, the same service philosophy used for adults applies. Although multigenerational interaction is *sometimes* good, it is important to provide a space where teens can take ownership and be free to behave in developmentally typical ways.

If older children frequently try to move into a teens-only space, it may be time to look at the spatial needs of older children. However, even if the children's section provides only for the needs of preschoolers, and nine-year-olds are not being served properly, the solution is not to supplant the needs of teen users.

TEEN SPACE IS NOT A MEANS TO SEGREGATE

A dedicated teens space is not an opportunity to enforce what Anthony Bernier refers to as "age apartheid." It is not a license for staff to segregate the teen population or to keep them away from adults who may find their presence distasteful (Bernier 2013).

Providing a dedicated space for teens in the library setting may be viewed as a means to solve the perceived problem of teens being present in the library by relegating teens to a single area. So while the result is a teen space the motivation for its creation may be a negative one—to segregate teens. A dedicated teen space shouldn't be considered a way to segregate teens from the "general population," but as a place to showcase teens' achievements and recognize their contributions.

THE TEEN SPACE IS NOT PROPERLY ACTIVATED BY STAFF

A library doesn't truly have a teen space if it does not have a teen services librarian. Up-to-date technology and nice furnishings are important, but the emphasis should be on experiences, not features. The features and even the space itself need a service context and like programming, creating a space merely for the sake of having a space is not an end unto itself. It is what happens in the space that is important. Experience trumps the fancy stuff. The staff is there to facilitate the experience regardless of any bells, gizmos, and whistles.

Funding for capital projects (e.g., building new facilities or renovating existing ones) is easier to find than funding for staff. If the library builds a teen space it is (theoretically) a one-time cost, whereas staffing the space with teen librarians entails recurring costs for salaries and benefits. Unfortunately, it is not uncommon for the library to build a teen space but not allocate funds to staff the space with teen services librarians and paraprofessionals. The most well-appointed teen space will turn into a wasteland if there isn't appropriate staff to activate it through programming or consistent engagement with teen users, but even the most humble teen space can function if there is teen services staff present to foster teen participation and engagement.

In instances where what might be considered problem behaviors take place in teen spaces (particularly those with specialized equipment) two questions can generally root out the problem:

1. Is there adequate teen services staff?
2. Do both older children and teens use the space?

Generally, if there is no staff to activate the space and assist teens, the space (and its specialized equipment) will feel as though it was just plunked down without service context. If there aren't dedicated staff members, and general staff just rotates through the teen space, there will be no opportunities for staff and teens to get to know each other. Consistency is also key in this situation.

If the space is open to older children, chances are that the expectation of the level and complexity of unmediated activities possible with this age group is not realistic. ("I can always tell when there's a ten-year-old in there, because they wind themselves up in the curtain that acts as a meeting space partition.")

There are situations where libraries have shut their doors during after-school hours because of teens or require teens to be registered by parents and to sign in and out of the library during each visit (Glick 2000), sign in and out of a dedicated teen space, or attend mandatory orientation with their parents before accessing specific features of a teen space.

In addition to real privacy issues, these types of registration require-ments serve as obstacles and barriers to teen access to the public library or portions of the public library. If teens must attend a library orien-tation with a parent to gain access to a portion of the public library building—that becomes a real obstacle to a teen who can't seek or get parental buy-in for their use of the library.

When library administration paints all teens as troublemakers, and threatens to deny them access to library services, it is a clear case of discrimination. Subjecting teens to a higher standard in order to access services or participate in activities—if they must attend an orientation, provide identification, register, or are otherwise subject to restrictions that do not apply to other population groups—constitutes a form of age-based apartheid. It is necessary to deal with individual cases of disruptive behavior. However, the library must examine whether its policies and procedures contribute to a situation where restricting access to an entire age group seems to be a reasonable remedy.

It's important to ask what the library hopes to achieve by imposing restrictions and requirements. Or, perhaps the real question is, what are they trying to prevent? If the library is trying to prevent a reoccurrence of something like damage to equipment or vandalism, it must determine what the circumstances behind the situation were, and what role library issues like space or staffing played. The library must remedy its role in contributing to the problem before imposing restrictions on teen users.

Shortly after opening, the Chicago Public Library's teen space, You Media, dropped its original requirement that teens attend an orientation before using sound-recording equipment, because they realized that teens wanted to use it immediately instead of waiting up to one week to go through a scheduled orientation. The library realized that teens were eager to begin experimenting and tinkering with the equipment. Those teens who had more than a casual interest were likely to return to attend advanced classes. Today's discourse about library service to teens emphasizes self-directed out-of-school learning, which requires dropping old attitudes about restricting resources to certain times or to an initiated few. The library must promote a teen services culture of *yes!*

Cast Out of the Garden

When young people age out of the teen library space, it is not uncommon for the transition to be difficult for both young adults and the teen services staff. Teens who have volunteered throughout all of their high school years, and have become fixtures in the teen services space, may feel abandoned when they turn nineteen. They may feel as though they are being cast out of a place where they forged relationships with staff, were integral in the development and implementation of programming, and were decision-makers about policy and service focus. They may feel they have been cast into a generic, impersonal service landscape.

The teen services librarians can be the mediators who help teens transition into adult services. They can make appropriate introductions and find volunteer opportunities for teens who wish to continue their service to the library.

The success of this transition is critical to the future of the library. If young adults are plunged into a landscape of impersonal features that have no context or connections, they may end their relationships with the library.

The teen space hasn't become an Eden because of its physical features. It has been crafted by staff who have practiced the living philosophy that teens are partners, cocreators, and collaborators who activate the space through the decisions they make and the interests they bring to the library.

Real-World Tactics:
Start with Bookshelves and a Book Cart

Bookshelves filled with YA fiction and a couple of chairs are not a teen space, but they're a start. Having YA material within reach of teens using the teen area is important to foster connection to the collection—but the primary purpose of a library teen space should not be the housing of materials. The purpose of the teen space is for it to be activated and inhabited by people (teens).

Even if a bookshelf is all there is to work with, it can be the basis for teens to take ownership and customize the space. Teen services librarians can devise ways for teens to mark their territory in the library using endcaps, bookshelves, and book carts to display items that invite teens to participate, linger, and customize their space. (Note the conscious avoidance of book reviews and name-your-favorite-book suggestions!)

Endcaps can:

- display teen artwork from programming or spontaneous creation
- advertise upcoming teen events and teen-created fliers
- showcase photos of past teen events

Bookshelves can:

- hold items created by teens
- display artifacts created during teen programming
- house a survey box, interactive poetry display, or a large-scale seek-a-word puzzle

Book carts can:

- be customized by teens with stickers and paint
- be used as workstations for teen volunteers
- house come-and-go activity supplies that teens can use to make items to post on the bookshelves and endcaps
- contain board games that invite teens to spread out and linger

When bookshelves and book carts contain supplies that teens can use creatively, activities can go on at any time, even if a teen services librarian isn't around or no formal activities are scheduled. Yes, this means leaving supplies out and unattended. Yes, it's all right to do that.

When teens and teen services staff activate a space it helps build a case that additional, more intentional space is needed to service the teen population of library users. The teen services librarian should view a bookshelf as a place from which to begin building an empire.

SOAP BOX MOMENT

How to Talk to Architects

After the teen focus groups, there will come a moment in any large-scale renovation or new construction of a teen space when adults (like architects and designers) take over. This is a critical point in the project and you are responsible for keeping the integrity of the teens' vision at the forefront of the design.

Because they are designing for teens, chances are the designer will create a "fun and funky" design certain to appeal to nine-year-olds and to appall seventeen-year-olds. It is perfectly all right to tell a designer that you hate it. (Try: "This design is way off track for what we need." "This design is too young for the target clientele." "This design would be more appropriate for children.") Remember you are representing the client group and the designer has heard far worse than anything you will say.

Understand that architects and designers speak a different language than we do—it is up to us to explain how the teen space will be used (i.e., form follows function) and its overall aesthetics. I've used descriptors like *high-end, elegant, sophisticated,* and even *expensive* to describe how a teen space should look and feel. Try this: Tell the architect the teen space should look like a Dolce & Gabbana boutique was dropped into the middle of a Walmart.

REFERENCES

Bernier, Anthony. 2003. "The Case Against Libraries As 'Safe Places.'" *Voice of Youth Advocates* 26 (August): 198–199.

Bernier, Anthony. 2013. *Transforming Young Adult Service.* Chicago: Neal-Schuman Publishers.

Bernier, Anthony, Michael Males, and Colin Rickman. 2014. "'It Is Silly to Hide Your Most Active Patrons': Exploring User Participation of Library Space Designs for Young Adults in the United States." *Library Quarterly* 84 (2): 165–182.

Bjørneborn, Lennart. 2008. "Serendipity Dimensions and Users' Information Behavior in the Physical Library Interface." *Information Research* 13 (4). www.informationr.net/ir/13-4/paper370.html.

Buckley, Donald. Personal correspondence. 2013.

Danish Agency for Library and Media. 2010. The Public Libraries in the Knowledge Society: Summary from the Committee on Public Libraries the Knowledge Society. www.kulturstyrelsen.dk/fileadmin/publikationer/publikationer_engelske/Reports/The_public_libraries_in_the_knowledge_society._Summary.pdf.

Forrest, Charles. 2009. "Academic Libraries as Learning Spaces: Library Effectiveness and the User Experience." *Georgia Library Quarterly* 46 (3). http://digitalcommons.kennesaw.edu/glq/v0146/iss3/4.

Gee, James Paul. 2004. *Situated Language and Learning: A Critique of Traditional Schooling.* New York: Routledge.

Glick, A. 2000. "The Trouble with Teens." *School Library Journal* 46 (10).

Hvenegaard Rasmussen, Casper, Henrik Jochumsen, and Dorte Skot-Hansen. 2008. Learning from Experience Economy—the Danish Way. Paper presented at the Fifth International Conference on Cultural Policy Research, Yeditepe University, Istanbul, Turkey.

Ito, M. et al. 2010. *Hanging Out, Messing Around, Geeking Out: Kids Living and Learning with New Media.* Cambridge, MA: MIT Press. https://mitpress.mit.edu/sites/default/files/titles/free_download/9780262013369_Hanging_Out.pdf.

Jenkins, Henry, Katie Clinton, Ravi Purushotma, Alice J. Robison, and Margaret Weigel. 2006. *Confronting the Challenges of Participatory Culture: Media Education for the 21st Century.* Cambridge, MA: MIT Press. https://mitpress.mit.edu/sites/default/files/titles/free_download/9780262513623_Confronting_the_Challenges.pdf.

Levien, Roger E. 2011. *Confronting the Future—Strategic Visions for the 21st Century Public Library.* ALA Office for Information Technology Policy, *Policy Brief* 4 (June). 2011. www.ala.org/offices/sites/ala.org.offices/files/content/oitp/publications/policybriefs/confronti ng_the_futu.pdf.

London, Rebecca, Manuel Pastor, Jr., Lisa J. Servon, Rachel Rosner, and Antwuan Wallace. 2010. "The Role of Community Technology Centers in Promoting Youth Development." *Youth and Society* 42 (2): 199–228.

Pine II, B. Joseph, and James H. Gilmore. 1999. *The Experience Economy: Work is Theater & Every Business a Stage.* Boston: Harvard Business School Press.

Sullivan, Louis H. 1896. "The Tall Office Building Artistically Considered." *Lippincott's Magazine* (March): 403–409.

Young Adult Library Services Association. 2012. *National Teen Space Guidelines.* www.ala.org/yalsa/sites/ala.org.yalsa/files/content/guidelines/guidelines/teenspaces.pdf.

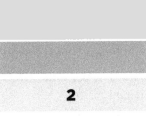

2

TEEN LIBRARY
PROGRAMMING

KEY CONSIDERATIONS

- Why does the library offer programming, events, and activities for teens?
- How does library programming fit into the broader service context?
- How can teen programming be initiated even when barriers are present?
- In what ways might teen programming failures of the past inform current resistance to teen programming?
- Why do teen services librarians plan programs that no teens attend?
- How is teen participation essential for effective teen programming?
- How does teen program planning differ from children's program planning?

A Service in Context

Although most library services are always available on-demand to teen customers (e.g., readers' advisory, the collection, etc.), programs and events for groups of teens are usually scheduled.

Like children's programming, teen programming is intended to meet the requirements of a patron group with unique needs and characteristics.

Unlike children's programming, teen programming:

- requires a different level of parental involvement
- has a shorter established history
- takes both new and traditional forms
- devises situations for teens to become decision-makers and program producers

The success or failure of a teen programming effort can depend on many factors, and there are a number of underlying causes that contribute to either outcome. Just as every community is unique, each set of circumstances that drives the success or failure of teen library programing is unique—there is not a one-size-fits-all formula for success.

Teen library programming is not an end unto itself. The goal of teen programming isn't attendance numbers. Programing that is divorced from service context will not move the library toward the realization of goals.

Service Instinct

If a library doesn't know *why* it offers teen programming (or why it doesn't), and hasn't defined program goals, how will it know if it's succeeded? Most organizations and people can describe *what* they do, but very few can articulate *why* they do it (Sinek 2009). The library needs to know why it offers an initiative or service, what needs it is trying to fulfill, and what it must achieve to determine whether or not it has succeeded.

Teen services librarians may know instinctively why teen programming is a core library service, but in the real world, where they must compete for resources, it is vital for them to go beyond anecdote and gut feelings. When speaking to the library's director, managers, and staff, library board members, city leaders, and community members, teen services librarians must be prepared to articulate a service rationale based on an understanding of community needs, and to back this up with examples of successful teen programs that meet the library's overall service mission and strategy.

No one questions the benefit of children's story time, and children's services librarians are not usually asked to justify or provide rationale for children's programming and activities. However, teen services librarians are often required to use youth development models to justify teen services and programming. Teen services librarians should be careful not to oversimplify or generalize when using the youth development models. They should avoid being put in a position to use models to prove concrete outcomes of teen programming.

Youth development models are not a justification for teen programming. In fact, justification for teen programming is unnecessary—the reason there should be programming for thirteen- to eighteen-year-olds is that programming is a core service of the library.

Barriers to Teen Programming

A variety of influences can impede the implementation and success of teen library programming efforts:

- Teen programming may not be considered a core service or priority in an organization.
- Teen programming efforts may have failed in the past.
- Teens may be considered a nuisance population, and offering activities for teens will serve only to attract more of them.
- Teens do not have a vocal constituency to advocate for them.
- Staff may have unrealistic expectations of teen programming results.

If a library is currently engaged in teen programming that is less than successful, it should stop and assess the contributing factors, which may include:

- the service community
- the current method of program development and implementation
- the manner in which existing programming aligns with the needs and interests of teens in the service area
- the level of teen involvement in the development and implementation of teen programming

Other barriers to teen programming may come from adult attitudes about teens and teen programming, past programming failures, the location and layout of the library, the level of funding, and the attitude and expectations of the teen services librarian.

ADULT ATTITUDES

Adult library users and library staff and management may openly complain about the presence of teens in the library, and they may particularly take issue with types of programming that attracts teens in groups. Adult library users and library staff members may have the attitude that all programming for teens must be "educational" in the traditional sense, or related to books and reading. Adult library users and library staff members may continue to espouse the traditional notion of the library as a quiet place, and contend that library programming for teens should be limited to quiet activities. Adult library users may express disapproval that their tax dollars are being used to provide a teen hangout or video game arcade.

The teen services librarian may be asked, "What does *that* have to do with the library?" Because teen programming may take nontraditional forms, they are sometimes perceived as not being library-related. For example, a group of teens playing a video game may cause a patron or staff member to question the validity of this type of program.

Even if coworkers do not influence whether or not teen programming is provided, their attitudes can influence others. If a member of the public asks, "Why are those teens playing video games in the library when they should be doing homework?" it matters how library staff members respond.

If a staff member agrees with an adult library user's complaints, it reinforces the negative perception of teen programming and of teens themselves. Regardless of personal opinions, ageism, like sexism and racism, must not be tolerated. This perception that staff should be free to criticize a library service for teens is rooted in the social acceptability of antagonism toward teens. These staff members don't have a problem with the general idea of programming—everyone agrees that children's programming is a core service—but they do with the age group who will attend the programs. Open criticism may be tolerated because managers or administration send a message (no matter how subtle) that teens are not valued. They may be considered unwelcome, or even feared. This disdain for teens can manifest as resistance to programming for teens. If the result of teen programming is that more teens visit the library, this outcome may not be seen as positive.

Administrative support is the best remedy for teen-resistant coworkers. If management emphasizes that teen programming is valid, a grumbler has no recourse. If the service landscape for teen programming isn't solid and lacks managerial support, an anti-teen staff member can erode potential support for the idea. To counteract this, the teen services librarian should make an effort to inform colleagues about teen events. The value of the teen services librarian's enthusiasm and positivity about the events should not be underestimated. The teen services librarian should also volunteer to give presentations about how teen programming helps meet organizational goals. She should not be shy about showcasing successful programming and to use attendance numbers (and even circulation numbers) to demonstrate how teen programming and services contribute to the overall vitality of the branch location.

Finally, the teen services librarian should not hesitate to communicate with her manager or administration if the attitudes of coworkers do not improve or are detrimental to teen programming efforts.

Although a teen services librarian may instinctively know the value of a seemingly nontraditional type of activity, he must be prepared to articulate its benefits. Just as children enjoy more than words, reading, and books at story time, teens learn social skills, bond with the library, and experience the library as a relevant place when they engage in so-called nontraditional library activities.

Persistently communicating the benefits of teen programs, and demonstrating how they align with the library's service mission, can preempt questions about their value. In addition to reporting attendance numbers and other statistics, teen services librarians should regularly produce narrative reports illustrating how teen programming efforts fit into the broader library service context. These reports should be produced even if managers do not request them. Teen services librarians can use them to communicate the current level of teen programming and assess its success by using metrics (rather than conjecture) about the outcomes of teen programming. Separately tracking teen programming statistics is particularly important in libraries where teen services and children's services statistics are combined into a single number.

PAST PROGRAMMING FAILURES

Teen services librarians may find themselves in a library system where there is little support for teen programming because it has failed in the past. It can be difficult to initiate teen programming efforts in a library with a history of unsuccessful teen services and a long memory. The response may be summarized as, "We tried teen programming a few years ago and nobody came."

Efforts to initiate teen programming in this service landscape may be seen as a waste of time. The expectation may be that any further efforts will fail. There are strategies that can be employed to ease teen programming back onto the service menu. A teen services librarian can ask teen regulars to plan a casual program for themselves and their peers (*casual* here is code for no cost). Teens can use resources already available at the library (e.g., chess sets or craft items), or can bring in items from home. These activities should seem spontaneous, and teen services staff should be standing by to record them with photos or video that can be used to demonstrate to library decision-makers that there is a need for teen programming. The teen services librarian should undertake such programming effort without seeking formal permission. Once a number of successes are documented, organizational memory will be of these recent, positive activities, not past failures.

LIBRARY LOCATION AND LAYOUT

The location of the library branch or the physical layout of the branch may be barriers to teen programming. The teen services librarian should assess a number of factors: the library's location and its proximity to schools and other teen gathering places; any public transportation barriers like a lack of bus stops; or physical barriers like highways, which prevent pedestrian access to the library.

Additionally, teen services librarians should examine the demographics of their libraries' service areas. Although librarians may know roughly how many teens they see in their own branch locations, looking at demographic information will help them assess how many teens in the community are not library users. Knowing the number of students in the service area's closest high school is a basic part of this community demographic portrait. School district information and census data will yield valuable insights about the library's teen users and potential users.

If teens are not visiting the library for programming, then the library can deliver programming to them. Moving programming for teens outside of the library may be the best way to deliver these services. This isn't the type of outreach designed just to inform teens about services available at the library location—it is the direct delivery of library service in off-site locations such as high schools, shopping malls, and community centers. Going to the places teens frequent allows for the direct delivery of library services while extending an invitation to teens to visit and become involved with their library.

When making contact with local high schools, teen services librarians should be sensitive to the possibility that a call from the public library with information about a teen service or program may be perceived by a high school librarians as yet one more thing to take on in addition to already overwhelming duties. Focus on what the library can do for the school—not what hoops the school might have to jump through to get students to use a service or program. Maybe the school librarian isn't the gateway to the students. Perhaps the art teacher or the apparel teacher may see the potential of a visit from the public library and be eager to have students engage in a library program, or contribute content such as artwork, poetry, or photographs to the public library's blog. Any contact with students in the school venue is an opportunity for them to begin forming a relationship with the library. The library might be out of their way, but teens may think it's worth the trip after they learn about resources and opportunities to volunteer, and other ways they can engage in meaningful participation.

The physical layout of the library can also be a barrier to programming. Teen programming may have to compete for use of a location's multipurpose room in a way that children's story time might not.

Recurring teen programming might be displaced from the multipurpose room and cancelled when the room is requested by other agencies, such as Library Friends and homeowners associations, or reserved for other library programming efforts. A willingness to bump teen programming is an indicator that it may be a low priority.

There is a way to assure teen programming always has a venue—hold it in the library's teen space or, in the absence of a teen space, designate a teen space for the duration of an activity, even if this is only a table on the general service floor.

Holding programming within a teen space has several benefits. It showcases positive teen activities; encourages casual teen users to join an activity without having to go into a separate space that might seem exclusive; helps teens take ownership of the space; fosters connections to the YA collection because of proximity; and allows teen staff to be essentially "on-desk" while also facilitating teen programming.

Although particularly sound-intensive programming might be difficult (but not impossible) to hold on the general service floor, there is no reason why teens can't gather to engage in a game or activity. A reasonable level of noise is to be expected when a group of people of any age gather. The teen services librarian can emphasize to managers that the activity will last only one hour, that teens attending library programming after school is positive, and that competition for the meeting room requires the use of an alternate space in the building.

FUNDING

Many libraries rely on fundraising entities like foundations or Friends of the Library groups to support library programming efforts. The competition for these funds can be a barrier to teen programming. Friends of the Library groups may direct funds for programming to children or senior citizens instead of teens. This may grow out of the perception that teen programming is not a core service, or from a lack of awareness about teen programming efforts or successes, or a distaste for certain types of teen programming (or teens themselves).

There are steps teen services librarians can take to assure that a Friends group is educated about the benefit of teen programming, beginning with communicating actual—not potential—positive results as a means to demonstrate its effectiveness. Teen services librarians should make the Friends group aware of the positive things teens are doing in the library by providing photographs, videos, and anecdotes via e-mail or print. If the Friends group is asked to be part of this type of success they may fund further concrete teen programming efforts.

If a Friends group withholds funds because it is uncomfortable with the idea of groups of teens using the library, the teen services librarian should encourage teens to request programming support directly from a Friends group at one of its meetings. If a Friends group holds functions like book sales or bake sales, a teen services librarian should work the event with two or three teen regulars (or members of the Teen

Leadership Council if there is one). The teens should clearly understand that the reason they are there is to demonstrate how teens are a positive presence in the library, and also so the Friends group may get to know the teens as people. Ideally, these same teens will be the ones who make requests for funds for programs, events, and equipment.

These activities should be formally documented in reports and publicized in any press generated from Friends-supported programming initiatives. A handwritten thank-you note to the president of the Friends group from a teen representative is essential. A display of gratitude is not just good manners—it is also politically smart.

The strategy expressed here is useful for building advocacy for teen programming, and variations of it can be employed with managers, administrators, and other funding or decision-making entities.

SELF-PERCEPTION OF TEEN SERVICES LIBRARIANS

Another barrier to teen programming may be a teen services librarian's self-perception of his role in teen programming. A teen librarian's perception of her role is reinforced by what she reads about teen library programming in professional literature. Typically, professional literature invites teen services librarians to place themselves centrally in a number of roles related to teen programming. This focus on the teen librarian as activator of teen programming can be detrimental to teen programming success.

These include the following:

Problematic Role: Librarian as Idea Curator/Selector

The literature on teen programming often focuses on the *what* of teen programming. Program and event ideas are offered without benefit of any service context. A librarian curates ideas for use by other librarians in teen programming settings, who in turn select from these ideas and implement them in their own library locations without considering the unique needs and interests of two separate communities of teens—those who frequent their neighborhood library and those who do not. The librarians who pick and choose from these menus of teen programming ideas engage in a guessing game about which programs might be of interest or benefit to a specific service population of teens.

Problematic Role: Librarian as Benevolent Granter of Opportunity

Some librarians may have fixed ideas about teen program development and implementation. The language used to discuss teen programming often emphasizes how librarians control teen programs that are "conceived" by librarians, who then "allow" teens to engage in a given activity. Librarians are the ones who decide when and how to get teens involved in a given activity (Sze 2012). The librarian is seen as the decision-maker and the activator of programming, without any input from teens.

Problematic Role: Librarian as Transferor of Appreciations

Another approach suggests that instead of relying on laundry lists of program ideas, librarians use their own interests and talents as sources for teen library programming ideas. There is a case for collaboration among public librarians that is based not only on shared professional interests, but also on personal interests, hobbies, and skills. Some practitioners suggest that librarians need to examine if they are capitalizing on their hidden strengths, interests, and skills (Spirito 2012). Although there are situations where it is appropriate for a librarian to employ personal interests and skills, in this approach the focus still remains on the librarian rather than on teens. Inherent in this role is an expectation that the librarian's interests and hobbies will drive the programming ideas that will be implemented for teens.

Optimal Role: Librarian as Facilitator/Activator

A less common approach advocates for librarians to involve teens in the decision-making about the programing. Tricia Suellentrop (2006) asks, "Isn't it time to give teens more power and control over their library experience?" She notes that direct teen input to program development is key to its success. The goal should be even more explicit and focused—creating an environment where teens' participation in the development and implementation of library programming for themselves and their peers is at the heart of successful programming. To achieve this, the teen services librarian should strive to be a facilitator/activator, with teens taking the role of innovator/implementer.

EXPECTATIONS OF TEEN SERVICES LIBRARIANS

The expectations librarians build about what and how teen programming *should be* can be a barrier to programming success. If a teen services librarian's vision of a program requires that a group of teens arrive on time, prepared (e.g., with the book read or the poem written, or set to listen to an adult speaker) and ready to engage in an activity according to a structured plan, the librarian may be setting himself up for disappointment—and potentially sowing the seeds of discontent with the idea of teen programming—because things seldom go exactly as planned. It is important to be flexible and accommodate the spontaneous evolution and improvisation that may occur during a teen program (e.g., a Perler beading activity can become a necklace-making activity). The teen services librarian may have actually witnessed a successful teen program, yet may feel disappointed because the program didn't go exactly as planned.

The ideal to strive for in teen programming is for teens to plan and implement programming ideas for themselves. In order for teens to take leadership roles, teen services librarians must understand that the specific program activity (the *what*) is not important. What is important—and unique and valuable—is that teens are fully in charge of an activity from selection to planning to implementation. The interaction (the *why*) between the librarian and the teens themselves is the aspect of programming with the greatest potential and importance. *What* is not as important as *why*.

AVOIDING PERSONAL REACTIONS

Teen services librarians may have personal reactions to low attendance and lack of interest in a particular activity because they invested time in the planning and promotion of a particular teen program.

In the following blog comments, teen services librarians express personal reactions to program failures.

> I had a program with a guest speaker—more than one, actually—
> and not a single person showed up. Embarrassing, but I moved
> on. . . . I had a book talk where one person came. A book talk
> about vampire books for 7–12th graders and it was a 5th grade

boy who came. We talked for 15 minutes or so, he told me what books he liked, and I was able to give him personal reader advisory. Then he went home with the grand prize of all the *Twilight* books. I just try to not take it personally . . . even though it's hard!

I take it personally even though I know I shouldn't! I realize they have lives and things to do but it's hard when I put time and effort into something. I will say, I'm glad I'm not alone. It seems no matter the size of the library system, there are always those programs that just don't bring in teens. (Kelly J. 2010, YALibrarianSarah 2010)

Teen services librarians must understand that programming doesn't have anything to do with their interests. It has to do with teens' interests. Ideally teens will take the lead in the development and implementation of library programming for themselves. When they take on authentic decision-making and implementation roles, there is no chance of zero attendance. Teen services librarians should focus their efforts on recasting teens from the role of patrons to those of partners and producers of teen programming.

Changing the Focus from Inward to Outward

When a group of teen services librarians get together and the topic of programming comes up, chances are they will begin to discuss which ideas work, which don't, which are on trend, and which can be done on the cheap.

The discussion can sometimes be very inward-facing: librarians will talk about what *they* like, what *they* are interested in, or what *they* think teens like or are interested in. Certainly, teen services librarians should discuss trends in YA programming among themselves, but this discussion often ignores the most important element—teens.

There are many sources of information about teen programming ideas, but librarians simply choosing ideas based on their own interests and preferences is not the best approach. The programming ideas found in books and on websites are valid and clever. But if a librarian selects a programming idea without involving teens, it cannot be considered a success—no matter how many teens attend—because the library has wasted an opportunity to engage teens meaningfully in the programming process. The goal is to have teen programming planned and implemented *by* teens, not *for* teens.

Parents ask *when* children's story time is scheduled, not *if*. Programming for children has become central to library service; it is an integral part of library activities (Sullivan 2005). Because parents may not understand or expect the library to offer library programming for their children once they turn thirteen and enter their teen years, they may not be vocal in their support or advocacy for teen library programming.

Librarians should not approach library programming for teens as they would library programming for children. Treating teen services as functionally the same as children's services can drive failure. The teen program planning model is vastly different from the children's program planning model.

Part of the role the children's librarians play is to plan story time and other early literacy and library events for a variety of age groups. These are well-defined activities with clear developmental goals. In the children's story time model, the librarian is, for the most part, the presenter/implementer and the children are the audience. The same model, where the audience are receptors, does not work as well for teens.

If teen services librarians are developing programming for teens in a silo—at an essential disconnect—they are not meeting the needs of the service population. Because developmental changes influence the interests and abilities of teens, many of them may not be interested in the kinds of programs that might have attracted them at earlier ages (Quinn 1999).

TEENS AS PRODUCERS OF LIBRARY PROGRAMMING FOR PEERS

Teen library programming is not an end unto itself; without service context it does not move the library toward the realization of the goal of teen participation in the planning and implementation of services and programming. Whenever possible, teens should lead the development and implementation of library programming for themselves and their peers. Teens should be the decision-makers and implementers, with library staff serving as facilitators who foster the teen-developed programming.

To achieve the ideal, where teens plan and implement library programming and activities for themselves and their peers, teen librarians must stop acting as program creators or selectors. Some teen librarians might find it difficult to relinquish this role. Planning programming is a creative and enjoyable activity. Giving this up means letting go of a fun part of the job, but the focus of professional satisfaction should be having teens engaged in developing and attending programs planned by themselves and their peers.

The RUSA/YALSA guidelines encourage the library to provide positive programming to meet the needs and interests of teens, as well as allowing them to experience ownership of the library and providing situations where teens can share their expertise and interests (RUSA/YALSA 2006).

PLANNING AND PARTICIPATION AS PROGRAMMING

When involving teens in program planning, the process of planning is more important than the program itself. The actual planning, organizing, and decision-making that teens engage in when developing an event qualifies as library activity (and should count as volunteer service hours). The planning sessions teens attend should be considered programs in and of themselves, which should be validated by collecting attendance numbers.

Planning can take place informally during conversations at the service point or in a structured teen leadership group. The notion of a teen group is not new. Many libraries use such groups to gather information about teens' programming interests. Nonetheless, librarians who seek programming input from a teen advisory group may continue to experience low or no attendance at the very programs the teens themselves suggested.

The notion of teens functioning in an "advisory capacity" is problematic. Consider the word *advisory*—it literally means having the power to make recommendations without necessarily having the power to enforce them. Soliciting programming ideas from a teen advisory group isn't all that different from consulting a list of teen programming ideas in a book. It is still inward-facing because it preserves the role of the librarian as the implementer/presenter of teen programming.

Teen programming efforts are most successful when teens are given responsibility over the resulting programming. Put simply, this is not a matter of gaining teens' buy-in or using them as a source of ideas for librarians to implement. When teens suggest an activity, and are put fully in charge of it, they are invested in the outcome and will work toward positive results like attendance at a program, the completion of a given activity, or the creation of a product. The responsibilities of a structured teen group should include the planning and implementation of programming for teens and their peers. To facilitate this reimagining, remove the word *advisory* and replace it with the stronger term *leadership*. It becomes the teen leadership group.

Excuses and Pitfalls

In an attempt to rationalize why teen programming is not successful or is not offered, teen services librarians and staff frequently find excuses for failures. They may decide that the teens in a given service population are over programmed, or that affluent teens don't need what the library has to offer. Institutional requirements that every teen activity must be educational, reading-based, and didactic; pitching teen programming to an inappropriate age group such as older children; or the existing procedures and organizational structures employed to plan programming for teens can also become pitfalls.

TEEN PROGRAMMING IS . . . FOR TEENS
NOT OLDER CHILDREN

The term *tweens* is often used to label older children who aspire to be like teens (Packaged Facts 2003). A new threat to the success of teen programming and services comes from the recent trend to include younger ages. Older children ages nine to twelve will naturally be drawn to teen spaces and programming; children and their parents will, unless prevented by staff, imperialize library spaces intended for teens. The same is true for programming.

Kay S. Hymowitz (2000) has noted that when marketers developed the term *tweens* to describe preteen consumers, it was a conscious nod to their teenage aspirations. Although the terms *teen* and *tween* are used almost interchangeably in professional literature, it's important to acknowledge that because tweens are actually still children, they have a vocal support group—their parents. They also have a unique set of developmental and service needs that differ from teens.

Teen services librarians may consistently be pressured to include older children in programs and activities for teens because the program topics will appeal to them. So why shouldn't preteens be allowed to attend? Nine- to twelve-year-olds should not be included in teen programming because the goal is to provide a forum where teens can take on responsibility for and make important decisions about the development and implementation of programs and activities for themselves and their peers. In many ways, what is happening during the program itself is secondary to the process.

Remember that the mission—the *why*—of teen programming is not to have high attendance numbers and packed meeting rooms, but to create a venue for teen participation, allow them to take leadership roles, and help them bond with the library. Letting older children attend teen programming may be a service to them, but it is a disservice to those who make up the target age group of teens.

If teen programming is taken over by older children, it ceases being teen programming. The same is true of teen programming that appeals to adults. Adults change the dynamic of social interactions, which will affect teen programs as much as if older children participate.

The fundamental assumption of the theory of social dynamics is that individuals are influenced by one another's behavior. Because of the established hierarchy, teens may defer to adults. This is why allowing adults (even parents) to attend teen programing will create a dynamic that inhibits the degree to which teens can exhibit normal teen behavior. Teen communities are important for identity development, a sense of belonging, and social support, regardless of whether or not they are mediated (Quan-Haase and boyd 2011).

"TWEENS" ARE THE ONLY PEOPLE WHO TURN UP FOR TEEN PROGRAMS

If teens stop attending, librarians may take this as a message that teens don't *want* library programming—and this mistaken assumption can lead librarians to shut teen library programming down instead of looking at the dynamics of what is being offered by the teen library program. Inviting ten-year-old girls and seventeen-year-old young men to the same program poses problems on a number of levels. The presence of both groups changes the dynamics and does not serve the needs of either. (A librarian in Texas began a secret second teen program after the advertised weekly teen library program was overrun with older children to the degree that teens stopped attending.)

The parents of older children are a vocal, built-in constituency who bring their own expectations and influences. Older children are more likely to *be taken* to the library (by parents)—whereas teens tend to *take themselves.* Because teens are independent and have more commitments and options about how to spend their free time, they are simply a more difficult group to attract. Therefore, it's especially important to hold the ground for teens. To make this absolutely clear, teen services librarians should unapologetically post "Teens Only" signs during programs, and "thirteen- to eighteen-year-olds only" when they list programs in the calendar of events.

The Wilmington Memorial Library in Massachusetts has a well-defined programming policy statement that deals with age ranges (www.wilm library.org/policies/programs). Although the statement doesn't specifically address tweens, it acknowledges that a public library may limit the attendance at programs to a specific age group based on developmental needs. In some cases, the nature and success of a program may require that attendance be limited based on age because programs are geared to a particular group's interests and developmental needs.

The Chicago Public Library offers "pre-teen" gaming programs and book clubs for children ages 9 to 12, which take place in the Children's Library (http://chipublib.bibliocommons.com/events/search).

The Boston Public Library defines the age groups for library programming as Children (subdivided into two groups: ages 0–5 and 6–12), Teens (ages 13–18), and Young Adult (ages 20–34) (www.bpl.org/programs/calendar.htm).

CENTRALIZED PROGRAM DEVELOPMENT

The participatory model of teen programming development and implementation is at odds with the centralized programming development model used by some library systems. As the name implies, centralized programming involves developing programming ideas at a single, central location for implementation in a library system's branch locations. Programs may be conducted by local branch staff or by programming librarians or paraprofessionals who visit the branch.

If centralized programming isn't working, it might be because this type of program planning doesn't fit activities into a broader service context and eliminates vital teen participation. Programming developed centrally without teen involvement can be inflexible and unresponsive to the spontaneous, evolving interests of teens. Centralized planning treats all teens the same, even though teens in different neighborhoods within the same city may have vastly different needs and interests.

Library systems that try to apply the centralized programming model for teens may find that teen programming is difficult to establish and maintain. The shortcomings of the centralized program planning method may result in low or no teen attendance at teen programs. This low attendance can be wrongly interpreted as teens not wanting teen programming rather than being attributed to a failure in the program planning method.

When teen programming has had several false starts, it is natural for teen services librarians to seek rationales for past failures and reasons not to pursue new initiatives.

"Teens in This Neighborhood Are Too Busy and 'Over Programmed' to Attend Library Programs"

Teen services librarians may reason that teens do not attend library programs because they already engage in many extracurricular activities and do not have time for library programming.

Perhaps past programming efforts did not meet the needs and interests of the teens in the service community. There are many opportunities in the community for teens to participate in activities, but there are few opportunities for teens to create and make decisions about or direct activities. A teen who plays football will not necessarily call the plays; a teen who plays in band may not be the conductor. However, the library can offer teens the opportunity to not only participate, but to define the form programming and activities take. This makes libraries a unique venue for teen participation in the community.

The library can be a venue that hosts the extracurricular activities in which the community's teens participate: a place where the National Honors Society or Model UN can meet, a worksite for science fairs, or a music performance space. The teen services librarian should talk to teens at the library or visit schools to determine their needs. A teen library leadership council that meets weekly or monthly at the local high school can plan activities that will achieve the same goals and benefits as those that take place in the library, but with the added advantage of having access to a concentrated group of teens in the school setting. This tactic may also be useful in communities where transportation to the library is an issue.

"The Teens in this Community Already Have All This Stuff at Home"

Teen services librarians may attribute the failure of teen programming to the affluence of the community in the service area. By reasoning that teens can acquire or already have acquired the things available to them at the library, the teen services librarian may be tempted to conclude that the library has nothing relevant to offer teens.

Beyond its implications for teen programming issues, such a conclusion is a serious indictment of the overall relevance of the library in the life of the community. Librarians should certainly consider what the library can offer in terms of technology as digital content becomes more personalized, portable, and ubiquitous.

The teens in a given service area may have access to the latest technology, but they may not have access to neutral space where they can freely congregate, and direct or engage in activities of their choosing and based on their interests.

It's not about the equipment or the program activities; it's about what happens at a program where teens are brought together in the library service context. Playing a video game with friends at home is a very different experience than playing a video game in a public place with new people. The library offers opportunities for teens to develop social competencies and skills as well as demonstrate mastery and achievement. This speaks to the evolving idea that the library is a community place—a space where people (in this case, teens) can come together and engage in planning activities, or work on independent or group projects.

"Every Program Is Related to Reading and Books"

Teen services librarians may be under the impression that all programming for teens must be book/reading-based. This may also be a directive from administration.

If the only programming on the teen services menu is book-based, this may give the impression to teens that reading is the only sanctioned activity in the library. Programming that centers on teens' interests (beyond reading) helps teens view the library as relevant and responsive. A library should reimagine its teen programs doing more than fostering a connection to the collection. If a teen picks up a book, that's great, but books shouldn't be the focus of the programming. Connection to the collection can be via a nonintrusive, temporary display of books and media related to the subject of the programming at hand.

Teens may suggest reading-based activities like book clubs because they fit into their interests. Book clubs that are developed and moderated by teens are a positive social way to explore and express their affection for books. Teen services librarians who have tried to establish book clubs may become frustrated when teens don't propose them. But, if a teen approaches the service desk and asks if there is a teen book club, the answer from the teen services librarian should be, "Yes, we do now, and you're in charge of it!"

"All Programs Have to Be 'Good for Teens'"

Adults know how to create a fun atmosphere for children's story time, but when those kids enter their teen years, adult opinions about what constitutes appropriate library programming may be informed by stereotypes. The library should not foster an atmosphere that espouses the notion that teens are in crisis or in need of guidance. To do so means that teen programming becomes didactic because it must demonstrate that it has "educational value." Outside agencies may urge library staff to present information about drugs, bullying, and gangs. Remember that this isn't school—participation in library programming is voluntary, and teens will most certainly vote with their feet.

IMMEDIATE PARTICIPATION:
FROM SMALL-SCALE TO LARGE-SCALE

Putting teens in decision-making roles regarding teen programming can involve small-scale participation or large-scale decision-making. Small-scale participation gives teens an immediate opportunity to direct an informal activity; larger-scale decision-making involves more ambitious programming efforts that can require weeks or months of planning.

Teen services librarians can begin building teen programming with small-scale participation, like asking teens who are already in the library for assistance with an activity. For example, in the case of an art activity, the teen services librarian should ask the first teen she sees to help her set out the supplies ("Would you put these on that table?") and immediately start talking about how the supplies will be used, and explain why she needs help (e.g., to make items to decorate the teen area). The program should just *begin*—no fanfare, no formality, no introductory speeches by the librarian about expectations or outcomes.

The goal is to begin putting the teens that are present in the library in charge of the activity. This means asking teens for assistance, seeking their opinions, soliciting advice, and asking them to suggest future activities. Librarians can begin building teen leadership in an unstructured, informal way by working through the following questions with teens:

> **"Which one of these should we do tonight?"** Asking which activity they prefer allows teens to set the immediate agenda—they are the ones who select what action will be undertaken.

> **"What should we do (tomorrow, next week)?"** This can be an open-ended question, or teens could select from a prepared list of choices.

> **"I really need some help. Can you help me out with (activity)?"** This acknowledges the need for the teens' participation, and that their contributions are valuable and necessary to the success of the activity.

Teen programming and participation do not have to be scheduled. A teen services librarian can take advantage of the presence of a group of teens in the library. When a librarian appears with a video game console and handful of cables and says, "Can someone help me set this up?

I don't know what I'm doing," he is acknowledging the expertise of the teens. Then, the librarian could hold up boxes and ask, "Which game do you want to play?" The next request should be for help—to set up a tournament, plan an open-play after-school event, or choose which new games to buy from whatever funds are available.

These are the first steps to begin engaging teens in the programming process. These first steps can be the start of establishing a teen group and growing teen programming. When teen services librarians 1) initiate contact with teens, 2) determine their interests, and 3) put them in charge of activities, they have begun the process that will involve teens in planning, forming groups, and expanding teen programming.

GIVING PROGRAMMING TIME TO GROW

When first developing teen programming, teen services librarians should acknowledge—and impress upon their managers—that any teen programming effort must be given time to grow. Teen programming isn't like story time. It is constantly in flux, subject to the interests and participation of the user group. It originates in the relationship the library builds with teens, and like any relationship, it needs time to grow.

Launching a teen leadership group or other programming initiative with an "event" may be a turn-off to teens and build unrealistic expectations on the part of the teen services librarian or administration. If few teens attend, this may leave a teen services librarian in an awkward position as they try to prove to managers the potential benefit and success of a teen leadership group. A teen leadership group or other programming initiative do not spring forth fully formed, but need time to grow and change according to the interests of the teens involved. The librarian must engage those who already visit the library to encourage them to become involved so they realize they have a say and can play a role in programming.

Successful teen programming depends on teen participation. There will be years when all the core teen planners and implementers graduate, and the following year should be considered a building year. This process is ongoing—it is not a perpetual motion machine designed to churn out traditional programming that doesn't change or evolve.

It is also the role of the librarian to seek out teens in the community and invite them to help with library programs and activities. Note they are not being asked to be a passive audience, but are being invited to play an active role in the production of library activities.

BUILDING CONSISTENCY BUILDS TEEN PROGRAMS

Rather than scheduling teen programming in a seemingly random way, it is vital to build consistency in a teen programming schedule.

Teen programming should take place at least once a week. Scheduling programming at the same time every week helps teens get into a routine—if they show up on that day and time there will always be something going on. Regularly scheduled programming will show colleagues that teen programming is a core service. Consistent scheduling also expedites the process of booking programming space.

The weekly teen program should be listed in the library's calendar of events with a generic description. Because a specific type of activity is not listed in the calendar, the focus remains consistent without locking down a predetermined series of activities. This allows the library to be nimble enough to respond to trends in popular culture and the interests and needs of neighborhood teens, so they can plan programs one or two weeks out, or even on the spur of the moment. Consistent scheduling, combined with increased teen participation in program planning, will help to increase attendance numbers.

Real-World Tactics:
Teen Library Programming Forms

Rather than concentrating on programming activity *ideas,* teen services librarians should familiarize themselves with certain *forms* of teen programming. These forms can be employed when setting parameters for teen participation. Specific program/event ideas/themes will ideally come from teens involved in the planning and implementation of programming for themselves and their peers. Teen services librarians can assess and apply the most appropriate program form to help achieve the desired program outcome. The programming form is *how* a program takes place. The form is the framework or structure of a program, rather than a topic or specific activity. For example, consider a craft program that teens can join anytime during its duration—make a bracelet and take it with them. Craft is the *type* of program, *bracelet making* is the *subject* or *activity* of the program, and make-and-take is the *form* of program.

The following examples are offered to assist teen services librarians in thinking about programming in a new way, in terms of form rather than specific activity.

Spontaneous/Impromptu

This form of programming is neither scheduled nor publicized. It takes advantage of occasions when teens happen to visit the library location. Staff approach teens and ask if they would like to assist with or engage in an activity. This type of program builds familiarity between teens and staff, and illustrates that the library recognizes and values teens. Approaching teens also allows the teen services librarian to begin growing a teen leadership group and to guide teens into the roles of decision-makers and implementers of programming. This also helps the teen librarian become aware of patterns of teen traffic in order to better schedule consistent teen programming.

Guerilla/Stealth

Like spontaneous teen programs, these programs aren't publicized or scheduled, but guerilla programs take place without the knowledge or approval of managers or library administration. This programming form is useful to help initiate teen programming in service environments where it is discouraged or simply not permitted.

The teen services librarian should work with teens in an unstructured, unscheduled way, and the program should appear to the casual observer to simply spontaneously happen.

Information about these unsanctioned programs is communicated by word of mouth by the teens that help plan and run the programs. This program form helps the teen services librarian demonstrate the need for teen programming in a given location.

The program results should be documented by the teen services librarian through photos for use with managers at an appropriate time.

Make-and-Take

In this program teens create or assemble a tangible item that they take home. This type of program works best with items that can be worn or can serve as gifts. Examples include bracelets, cellphone charms, buttons, or picture frames. Creating the item provides opportunities for teens to demonstrate competence and achievement. When teens show their creations to peers and talk about how they made them in the library, it promotes a positive image of the library.

Make-and-Leave

As the name implies, make-and-leave programs are those where teens make an item to leave at the library for the purpose of personalizing or decorating the teen space or other area of the library This type of program has the added result of teens customizing and taking ownership of the library's teen space.

Small-Scale Recurring

Teens plan and implement small-scale programs, which include leadership group meetings and interest-based activities that occur on a regular basis (e.g., weekly on the same day of the week and time of the day). Small-scale means a program that fits in the branch's meeting room or teen area. These small-scale activities can be planned days in advance and are publicized by the library and also by the teens in their schools or among a group of friends. This activity can be linear (i.e., with a beginning, middle, and end), like a movie or presentation, or cyclical (i.e., the activity can be joined at any time and can be repeated as desired) like open play of a game or a make-and-take activity).

Large-Scale One-Off

In contrast to small-scale recurring events, these events are on a larger scale. Teens may spend weeks, or even months, planning them; they may involve a partner agency or community group;

and they may possibly take place at a centralized location such as the main branch library to accommodate a greater number of teen attendees. A large-scale program may be supported by system-wide promotion, but like small-scale programs, large-scale programs are also promoted by the teens who planned them. Large-scale programs do not occur frequently, and may be one-time or annual events.

There are several things to keep in mind in terms of program development for teens.

Get in a groove with the teen programming schedule. *What* isn't as important as *when*—and when should be easy to remember. Resist the temptation of difficult-to-remember "Third Thursday"-style scheduling. Keep things on a weekly basis—and schedule a weekly program on the same time on the same day of the week. Teens will get to know that if they show up at the library on the designated day at the designated time, they will find something they can join in on.

Understand that although the teen programming schedule should always be consistent, it will vary depending on whether it's the school year or summer. During the school year, avoid obvious conflicts: if the local high school's basketball or football games conflict with the library's teen program night, then change the teen program night. Know the local high school's dismissal time and consider the types and schedules of available transportation, and set a realistic time for library programs to begin. Teen programming should be scheduled based on what's convenient for the teens. The program schedule should never depend on the library staff's dinner or desk schedule.

Use the after-school rush. Be aware of the teen traffic patterns at the library location. Is there an after-school rush? Are there days of the week when teen traffic is heaviest? The after-school rush is the best time to begin offering activities—the teens are already there. Get them busy planning and helping with activities, right there on the spot (even if the activities are not on the calendar). Ask them to come back because the library needs their help; after all, they are the experts on teen interests.

SOAPBOX MOMENT

Zero Attendance Is No Deterrent

I finally cancelled my teen book group because there was so little interest. After six years of trying, maybe only eight teens ever attended.

Rather than asking, "What is wrong with the programming?," this librarian has, in effect, asked, "What is wrong with these teens?"

Don't blame a customer who isn't interested in what the library wants to sell— if the library were a business it would quickly go bankrupt. But unlike a business, the library has the strange luxury of continuing to offer products that customers simply don't want. Persistence is a good thing—stubbornness is not.

When promoting teen programming, fliers may seem like an obvious option but relying on them as the sole means of promotion is naïve. Creating a flier, printing it out, and placing it on a service desk will not attract new users or program attendees. This is the library equivalent of preaching to the choir. If a flier is made (or even better, if a teen creates it), the teens who have planned the program should hand them out to their friends at school, or at places like the local skateboard or comic store. Directing teen programming information to adults via fliers or the library's web-based calendar of events isn't the same as targeting the information directly to teens. The goal is to have teens promote teen-created programming to their peers via word of mouth and social networking.

What if the library doesn't have any teen traffic? It's important not to make assumptions about the teen demographics of the community based solely on the teens that pass through the library's doors. The librarian may have to go out and find them. The teen services librarian should arrange to conduct an activity someplace other than the library as a means to meet teens in the service area. Don't confuse this with traditional informational outreach; rather, it is the off-site delivery of a library service.

BETWEEN ART AND SCIENCE

Scheduling consistent teen programming is more art than science. Giving a programming schedule enough time to become established is essential, but a willingness to adjust the schedule is also vital. Making too many adjustments may confuse teens. Making too few adjustments may waste valuable time and opportunities. Teen services librarians are urged to take risks, be flexible, maintain their sense of humor, and trust their instincts.

REFERENCES

Quan-Haase, Anabel, and danah boyd. 2011. "Teen Communities." In George Barnette, ed. *Encyclopedia of Social Networks*. Edited by George Barnette. London: Sage.

Hymowitz, Kay. 2000. "Girls' Sexy Aspirations Are Marketers' Target." *Philadelphia Enquirer*. October 7.

J. Kelly. 2010. Comment on "Teen Programs: A One Person Game." *YA Librarian Tales* (blog). December 15. www.yalibrariantales.com/2010/12/teen-programs-one-person-game.html.

Packaged Facts. 2003. *The U.S. Tweens Market.* 2nd edition. New York: Market Info Group.

Quinn, Jane. 1999. "Where Need Meets Opportunity: Youth Development Programs for Early Teens." *Future Child* 9 (Fall): 96–116.

RUSA/YALSA Joint Task Force. 2006. *Guidelines for Library Services to Teens.* www.ala.org/rusa/resources/guidelines/guidelinesteens.

Sinek, Simon. 2009. *Start with Why: How Great Leaders Inspire Everyone to Take Action.* New York: Portfolio.

Spirito, Phil. 2012. "Innovate and Collaborate for Success." *Public Libraries* 51 (3): 9–20.

Suellentrop, Tricia. 2006. "Letting Go." *School Library Journal* 52 (May): 39.

Sullivan, Michael. 2005. *Fundamentals of Children's Services.* Chicago: ALA Editions.

Sze, Lian. 2012. "Programming that Packs the Place." *Public Libraries* 52 (July/August): 14–16.

YALibrarianSarah. 2010. Comment on "Teen Programs: A One Person Game." *YA Librarian Tales* (blog). December 15. www.yalibrariantales.com/2010/12/teen-programs-one-person-game.html.

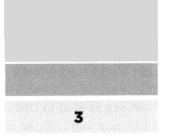

3

CRAFTING SERVICE DYNAMICS AND MODELING SERVICE STRATEGIES

KEY CONSIDERATIONS

- How can the attitude and actions of teen services librarians shape the teen services dynamic with colleagues?
- What steps can be taken to make sure the library doesn't seem unwelcoming and teen users aren't made to feel stupid or intimidated?
- How can staff approach and engage teens in conversation that leads to service interactions?
- How can teen services librarians help improve the service delivered to teens by all library staff members?
- How do staff expectations play a role is shaping service dynamics with teens?

Know Yourself, Know Others

Ideally, the teen services librarian acts as advocate, interpreter, public defender, counselor, mentor, and role model for both teens and colleagues. For the teen services librarian, understanding coworkers, teen users, and, of course, her own personal service style and possible prejudices is key to making a teen patron's experience of the library a positive one. To paraphrase the *Art of War:* know yourself and know others, and you cannot be defeated.

As well as acting as advocate for teen users, the teen services librarian is also a resource for colleagues, who helps them to build the professional skills and understanding needed to effectively provide service to teens. The teen services librarian must take an active role in crafting the service dynamics of the library for its teen users. This means fostering positive working relationships with even the most teen-resistant colleagues, managing positive and negative expectations, employing interpersonal skills, and cultivating opportunities for colleagues, managers, and administrators to understand how valuable and vital the presence of teens is to a thriving library location.

LIBRARY ANXIETY IS REAL

Constance Mellon (1986) coined the term "library anxiety" to describe the feelings of fear and discomfort undergraduate students experienced when using the library. Her research detailed a phenomenon where university students were intimidated by the library and library staff members.

The study described some primary reasons for experiencing library anxiety, including:

- being intimidated by the size of the library
- lacking knowledge of where everything was located
- not knowing where to begin or what to do (Mellon 1986)

Subjects were also afraid to seek help from library staff members. What a Catch-22! Not knowing were to begin, but not asking for help. Sound familiar? What was true for the undergraduate students in Mellon's study is most certainly true for teens. Teens may enter the library anticipating a bad experience—this could be based on past experience or from the concern that they do not know how the system works.

The teen services librarian should consider the role the library plays in creating an unwelcoming, confusing atmosphere that serves only to reinforce teens' fears. Part of advocating for teens is being aware of situations where the library uses jargon, is unnecessarily complicated, or is staff-focused rather than patron-focused. Why on earth would teens, who have a range of places to spend their free time, frequent a library that seems as though it intentionally orchestrates negative experiences and refuses to respond to their needs?

SERVICE POINTS AND STYLES

Teen services librarians need to understand how teens choose to use the library, how they seek information, and how they respond to the service schemes and patterns established by the library.

In the library there are teens who are hunters and teens who are gatherers—what and how they seek differs. The library must be responsive to teens' different styles. Hunters know what they are looking for; gatherers browse and see what they can find. Neither may know where to begin, especially if they are intimidated by a system that may seem designed to make them feel stupid. They won't want to ask for help if they feel as though the staff doesn't want to be bothered, or if they've previously felt discouraged when they've asked questions.

Gatherers may want privacy and peace to look around in the collection and discover things that appeal to them; hunters arrive with specific needs, or in search of a specific resource. In either case, the placement of the service point can hinder or facilitate the interaction between teens and library staff. Beyond the dynamics of where the service point is located, the most important feature of the service offered in the library is the library staff and the dynamic their attitudes foster in the space.

Teens learn not to ask questions. It doesn't matter where the service point is located if it is made unwelcoming by the attitude of staff. A current teen services librarian remembers an experience from her own teen years: "There was one librarian who was not friendly and clearly gave off a-don't-bother-me vibe. My brother and I learned not to ask questions when he was at the reference desk."

The staff member in this situation may or may not intentionally mean to seem indifferent or threatening, but he was undeniably unapproachable. This is a job performance issue.

When teens walk into the library they receive cues about library service. The jargon used to describe the typical service points is confusing—the terms *circulation* and *reference* are not very meaningful to many users. The placement of the service desk—its very approachability—sends signals about the library's service style and of its opinion about teen users.

Service Point as Barrier to Service

A service point (e.g., the information or reference desk) must be situated so that it becomes an obvious place to go to seek help. Too often, it becomes literally an obtrusive physical barrier to customer service.

Start with the premise that teens may not *ever* approach the service desk, and add that to the complications and considerations inherent in common placement models.

Many typical placement styles position a service desk in the teen space, which offers a service point in the teen space but screens it off, or put the designated service point for teens in the children's area. Although the most obvious placement of a service point for teens may be in the teen area, this may not work. In reality, many libraries do not have the resources to staff an age-specific desk whenever the library is open. A service desk that takes up space in the teen area might often be unstaffed. And, when it *is* staffed, teens may feel like they are being watched, or that they are occupying the adults' workspace. Having an adult staff member plunked at a service desk in the teen area (particularly if the teen area is small) may intimidate teens.

To compensate for a service desk that imposes on teen space, the impulse may be to make it more unobtrusive by literally placing it behind a screen, perhaps even a bead or metal-mesh curtain or a glass door. The intention may be to create separation between the service desk and teen space so that staff can be in the space without dictating or changing the dynamic. However, the resulting effect in libraries that have employed this is akin to putting a private office in the teen space. Teens may not be comfortable crossing a barrier to get to where an adult is sitting at a desk behind a computer. They may feel like they are interrupting if they need to ask questions (which they may suspect are stupid and annoying).

Some libraries, particularly those where teens services is combined with children's services, designate the children's services area as the service point for teens. The library may think that teens should use the children's desk, but that doesn't mean teens will choose to use it. Teens don't see themselves as children, and may not approach a service desk modified in height to accommodate transactions with children.

The form of the service point itself drives the service style promoted by the typical placement of the service desk. Rather than the arrangement of the service desk driving the type of service offered there (and perpetuating a barrier), the desired outcome of library service should drive the form of the service point. Form should follow function and promote rather than inhibit the desired outcome of providing service to teens. Given teens' reluctance to approach it, the usefulness of a service desk regardless of its location should be reevaluated.

This is an instance where the library can learn from and emulate a retail model. In high-end department stores, departments aren't staffed by personnel at fixed stations. Sales people stay on the service floor so they can approach customers, while staying in proximity to a service point needed to complete transactions.

Because teens may feel that they're not supposed to "bother" the adults, staff should initiate interactions with teen patrons rather than sitting passively at service points and waiting for teens to approach and ask questions.

Ideally, *every* member of the library staff is friendly and approachable. They proactively approach teens with friendly expressions, and . . . what? This is the critical moment—the point when first impressions are made.

First Contact: "May I Help You?" Does Not Work

Teens may not know what is on the service menu, so asking, "May I help you?" doesn't offer any clues to any sort of protocol or possibilities. This may lead teens to respond with an automatic, "I'm just browsing." And no, they don't necessarily mean it the way librarians do.

Asking a teen if you can help them is a quiz that is tantamount to an interrogation. If teens don't know what products and services are available, they don't know what to ask for, or even what the proper protocol for asking questions is. This is when soft-sell retail techniques can help: initiate casual conversation that can, if necessary, transition into a discussion about library products and services. "May I help you?" is too easy a request to turn down, thus stopping any conversation:

(Q: May I help you?) + (A: No.) = End of interaction.

This is another instance where the library can learn from retailers. In high-end retail establishments, chances are the salesperson will talk to customers about the weather or compliment the customer's outfit before getting around to any discussion about what the customer is looking for. Engaging in a conversation makes it more difficult for customers to offer the single-word answer "No." that will end the interaction. This technique is intended to make customers comfortable, to break the ice, and make sure people feel welcome and "fancy enough" to be around expensive merchandise. The same method helps make teens feel comfortable and able to express what they need.

This interaction in the library can begin with something as simple as "I really like your glasses (backpack, sneakers)." Or "Is it still raining outside?" This human approach acknowledges teens as individuals; conversation about library services and books will follow. The important thing for staff is to approach each teen with interest, kindness, and a positive, open demeanor. Emphasizing that the teen is welcome will counteract any fears he may have about being in an unfamiliar place where the staff act indifferent or superior and the rules are difficult to discern.

Helping Staff Effectively Serve Teens

Because the teen services librarians must be the lead advocates for teen services, they are called upon to do many things beyond the direct delivery of library services. They must also consistently model outstanding service strategies for their colleagues.

Regardless of their individual comfort level or desire to work with teens, all staff members at the service desk should be able to provide a basic level of effective service to customers of any age.

Some librarians seem to possess a natural rapport with teens, but others project obvious discomfort. When a child approaches the reference desk, staff members are, for the most part, capable of recognizing they should modulate their conversation level to match the developmental age of the child. With teens, pinpointing this level can be much more nuanced. Even if he looks like a grown man, a sixteen-year-old boy with five o'clock shadow is developmentally still a teen. Just as teens may not be equipped with the knowledge of how the library works, librarians may not possess the knowledge or professional skills to effectively serve teen library users. This lack of skill and understanding may manifest as fear and hostility toward teens and, by extension, teen services.

CRAFTING A POSITIVE TEEN SERVICES IMAGE

Teen services librarians must communicate a positive teen services message to all levels of the organization; part of doing this involves establishing and maintaining functional professional relationships with colleagues and coworkers. It is not uncommon for teen services librarians to sometimes feel at odds with colleagues, or fail to understand why some coworkers are not "teen people." If staff and colleagues see teens as a nuisance, then the efforts of the teen services librarian may be perceived as a means to attract more problem patrons. This can cause conflict and stress in the organization.

When working with teens, teen services people understand that there is a type of professional demeanor necessary to deliver effective service; it is pleasant, calm, and neutral. This attitude extends to coworkers, too. It's necessary to put on a professional game-face when working with teens *and* when interacting with colleagues. The conscious choices teen librarians make to communicate positively with coworkers, the language used to express teen services issues, and the teamwork and optimism exhibited must be deliberate and have service improvement as a goal. These soft skills are important in any job situation, but can be especially useful by assisting colleagues to appreciate teens and teen services—which will help teen services librarians improve the service environment for teens.

MODELING SERVICE STRATEGIES

When teen services staff is at the public service desk they have two service audiences: the people they serve (teens) and the people they serve alongside (colleagues). Teen services librarians know that information literacy and digital literacy opportunities are embedded in reference and readers' advisory transactions with teens. Simply narrating the steps they are taking as they search the catalog with a teen helps convey information about the skills necessary to conduct a successful search. The same is true with coworkers, who by osmosis can pick up service skills by observing the deliberate, subtle, or not-so-subtle steps taken by the teen services librarian. Being at the service desk with a colleague who lacks the capacity to serve teens well is a prime opportunity to model outstanding teen service for colleagues.

Instant replay: Recap the teen service delivery technique

The teen services librarian can routinely conduct a review of a completed service transaction for the benefit of a colleague. After a readers' advisory interview with a teen the librarian can recap the strategies she employed during the interaction: "I asked the teen what types of books they *don't* like rather than what types of books they *do* like because it is often easier for people to articulate what they don't like—that way we can better narrow down what they might like."

The teen services librarian should offer this recap spontaneously, without invitation or explanation. This technique should become part of the teen services librarian's on-desk routine.

Talk to colleagues

When speaking with colleagues about service strategies for teens, the teen services librarian should be specific and offer concrete suggestions. Sometimes it is difficult not to step in when a colleague is struggling to conduct a reference interview with a teen. Although the impulse might be to not interrupt the interview and potentially offend the colleague, this potential offense must be weighed against the importance of providing high-quality service to teens.

After the colleague completes the transaction, the teen services librarian should broach the subject directly and neutrally: "I noticed that sometimes when dealing with teen patrons you use a lot of jargon that teens might not understand. Like, you kept saying (state the jargon used). Next time, try explaining it this way—and it might be clearer for the teen." The comments should be framed so it's clear that the problem isn't that the staff member is using the wrong words, but it's the teen that needs help.

Demonstrate benefit

The teen services librarian can create opportunities for colleagues to see the benefits of teens in the library (e.g., as volunteers or program developers). If teens are contributing to the calm operation of the library, or if they are helping to accomplish tasks and serving as volunteers, it should be documented and recognized. Tracking the number of teen volunteers and teen volunteer hours on monthly or quarterly reports is vital.

Administration will particularly see the benefit of teen services when kudos comes from outside of the organization. A photo of a teen program in the local newspaper, or a letter from a community partner or school, may have far more value than an internal narrative or statistical report from the teen services librarian. The success of teen services rubs off on the entire organization.

Build allegiances

A powerful way to build allegiances between staff and teens is to introduce teen regulars and volunteers to staff. Giving reluctant staff members the chance to build a positive relationship with a teen volunteer can change their attitude toward teen patrons (Houston 2011).

Offer to conduct training

If it is possible to conduct training at a staff meeting, the teen services librarian should take advantage of the opportunity. Training is a large component of in-house advocacy. Getting colleagues on the same page regarding teen services so that all staff members use the same language and consistently apply rules and service techniques will benefit everyone—the whole staff, teen services librarians, and teen patrons. This also keeps teen services on the radar of managers in a positive way. It is a means to address issues in the location in a structured, nonconfrontational manner.

Talk to a supervisor

If a colleague interferes with the delivery of service to teens, this situation may require the intervention of a manager. Expressing concerns frankly and without emotion can be challenging, but a scientific detachment is necessary. Every person on staff must have the same goal of providing outstanding service to all library visitors, regardless of age. This is not about personalities; it's about everyone on staff delivering a high level of service to all patrons.

Teen Services Staff:
Serendipity versus Standard

Library systems that combine teen and children's services into "youth services" may face unique challenges when serving teens. Youth services often has a focus on children, and the term "youth services" becomes code for children's services (just as "family programming" is code for children's activities). In this situation, the lion's share of resources and effort may be dedicated to the very important work of providing outstanding library experiences for young children and their parents or caregivers. The perceived demand is strongest for services and programming for children. Children have the strong constituency of parents, who demand and expect children's services and programming (e.g., story time). Children's and teen services are not at odds with each other. Teen services is where children's services pays off.

Having staff positions in the organization with the job title "Teen Services Librarian" is important to the institutionalization of teen library services intended for thirteen-to-eighteen-year-olds. Libraries may recognize the need to provide specialized services for teens, but without dedicated teen services staff, the responsibility can be a hot potato that no one on the youth services staff is eager to catch. As a result, services and programming for teens can be left to chance or subject to the whims and interests of existing staff.

It is not uncommon to hear managers say, "Well, so-and-so used to do the teen program but she left and no one else wanted to do it."

The library may already employ youth services staff capable of and interested in serving teens, but leaving teen services to serendipity is not an effective service strategy to assure consistent service to this age group. If someone in the youth services cohort is good at and passionate about serving teens, teen services may blossom. However, if she leaves the organization there will be no mechanism or process in place for continuing service to teens. The person hired to fill her position may or may not have the capacity, interest, or desire to serve teens.

Service to this important user group can't be left to chance or be based on the individual interests and desires of staff members. Service to teens must be standardized and supported by dedicated staff positions with specific, teen-focused job titles. A dedicated teen services staff member not only ensures consistent delivery of service for teens, but also maintains viable levels of:

- advocacy for teens in the organization and community
- programming for teens
- partnerships with other youth-serving agencies and schools
- relationship building with teen users
- responsibility for activation of teen space
- modeling of customer service strategies for colleagues

Real-World-tactics: Readers' Advisory Tips

One of the specialized skills that a dedicated teen services librarian can bring to an organization is the ability to conduct readers' advisory with teen patrons.

This discussion of readers' advisory is offered with a caveat: this is about people—not books. Although it is important to have an understanding of teen resources, traditional library school curriculum places great emphasis on the YA canon and producing "book talks," as if these are paramount public-service benchmarks. Consequently, some teen services librarians earn their degrees equipped with a broad knowledge of YA fiction and authors, but with limited understanding of the client group they are tasked to serve. This is about teens, not titles.

When a situation arises where teen librarians are asked to offer readers' advisory to teens, there are a few things to keep in mind:

Don't gush. When doing readers' advisory, it can be hard not to gush when recommending books, but keep in mind that teens will naturally be skeptical about any title that the (insert gently pejorative descriptor here) librarian thinks is any good. If the librarian likes the book, how can teens believe it will be remotely of interest to them? Yes, there may be teens eager to talk about books with the librarian, but this isn't about what the librarian likes. If the librarian raves about a book and it sounds stupid to the teen, the teen will not trust anything the librarian says about any book.

Don't push. Teens may feel obligated to check out books the librarian suggests (because the librarian keeps saying how good they are!). A soft touch is the best approach. Keep things moving in a chatty way—without physically forcing a book into the teen's hands. Pulling a book off the shelf and then placing it cover-side up allows the teen to pick it up if she wants to, without feeling obligated to take what is handed to them. This technique keeps the exchange physically neutral and allows teens to make selections independently.

Be neutral. Tell a bit about the plot. Don't go overboard with superlatives. Remember this is not an opportunity to showcase book-talk expertise. Ask, "Does that sound like one you'd be interested in? You're not going to hurt my feelings if it doesn't sound good: I didn't write it." Then give a cue with a laugh and smile. Or try, "It's up to you. If you want to give it a try, remember that if you don't like it you don't have to finish it." In this way the librarian defers to the teen's individual tastes and opinions by letting him know it is okay if he doesn't love every book in the library. The librarian makes it clear that the teen's preferences and ability to make choices are respected.

Focus on the teen, not the parent. Always talk to the teen, even if the parent is asking the question. The parent may approach the desk with the (visibly uncomfortable and embarrassed) teen in tow and say, "He needs a book to read." The teen librarian should address the teen directly by making eye contact and introducing himself to the teen. Some parents will try to mediate this transaction, either because of reliance on the parent-child dynamic, or because the teen is reluctant to read. Keep the attention focused on the teen and what they like (or, perhaps more importantly, what they don't like). This is a conversation about the teen's interests, not about books. Ask, "What do you like to do?" or "What are you interested in?" *not,* "What do you like to read about?"

Do follow-up. Before the teen leaves, the teen services librarian should invite the teen back to discuss the success of the book selection process saying something like, "When you come back next time let me know if you liked any of those, okay? My name is . . . ." This is a way to forge a connection among the teen, the library, and the collection and demonstrate that the teen's tastes and opinions are valued and of interest to the librarian.

Teens, Not Titles

Time and again when I interview candidates for teen services positions, they go gooey for John Green but are at a loss regarding the target service population. (No, I don't want to hear your booktalk.) If you want to be a literature critic, go be a literature critic. A teen services librarian job is about serving teens and understanding the possibilities of the public library. The focus must be on the teen patrons served–not a fetishizing of the book and worship of the author. (Nothing personal, John.)

REFERENCE

Mellon, Constance. 1986. "Library Anxiety: A Grounded Theory and Its Development." *College and Research Libraries* 4 (2): 160–16.

4

RULES, CONDUCT CODES, AND BEHAVIOR

KEY CONSIDERATIONS

- How can staff's response to problem situations escalate those situations?
- What visual cues can be used to help teens feel welcome in the library?
- How can library rules be communicated to teens via the library's physical space?
- How are library rules developed and applied?
- Should there ever be different rules for different user groups or spaces?

The Library Code of Conduct versus Teen-Patron Code of Conduct

Like all library staff, teen services librarians must be aware of the Library's Code of Patron Conduct. But teen services librarians must view such policies from the viewpoint of a teen advocate. They need to be alert to both overt and subtle inequalities in the existence and application of rules spelled out in the Code of Conduct as they relate to teen patrons.

Teen services librarians must be keenly aware of any of the library's rules, procedures, and penalties that seem to be based solely on the age of patrons, or of separate sets of rules that impact teens in designated spaces. Teen services librarians must work proactively to assure that teens are being treated equally. They need to understand the role staff response plays in the ultimate outcome of these situations, and must model effective tactics for mediating problem situations that may arise with teen patrons.

Teen services librarians must be involved in the process of setting policy and drafting codes of conduct and behavioral guidelines. Although this may mean offering unsolicited input about current organizational practices to managers and administrators, it provides an opportunity to demonstrate critical thinking skills and to advocate for the target service population. Crafting behavioral guidelines helps to create a service atmosphere that emphasizes fairness, consistency, and kindness in interactions with teen patrons.

WHO THE RULES APPLY TO

Many libraries have established Codes of Patron Conduct that spell out the expectations, rules, and consequences of negative or restricted behaviors that patrons may engage in at the library. Although this Code of Conduct applies to everyone in all parts of the library (e.g., no hitting, pushing, or wrestling), some libraries choose to enforce a separate Teen Code of Conduct or an additional set of rules, which teens are expected to learn, understand, and follow, in addition to the general rules.

Sometimes rules not included in the formal Code of Conduct are posted to inform patrons about specific procedures or activities. This separate set of rules is often associated with a particular area of the library; for example, they may pertain to a particular space rather than to a particular age group. In this way, inconsistencies in the way rules are applied to different patron *groups* are cloaked by rules designated for different library *areas.*

A separate set of rules for the teen space, and by extension for teens, may indicate that teens are treated differently than adults or that there are different expectations placed on how they behave in the library. When a group of teens assembles in the library, some librarians may automatically expect them to be trouble:

> Such groups are usually regarded as rowdy or likely to become
> rowdy, and staff energy primarily goes toward controlling them
> rather than assuming such groups are normal and planning for
> them. The irrational assumption that a group of healthy ado-
> lescents should behave like shy, friendless, hearing-impaired
> seniors is rarely questioned. (Chelton 2002)

This desire to control teens with rules can lead librarians to develop complicated rules. If the library does post rules for the teen space they should be simple and direct to avoid ambiguities that invite debate. Jones and Shoemaker (2001) suggest keeping library rules minimal and simple: respect yourself, respect others, and respect property.

COMMUNICATING THE RULES

It's crucial that libraries carefully consider how they use signs. Posting rules should not be done in a way that makes library policy seem arbitrary or discriminatory. The benefit of having the behavioral guidelines posted is that staff may conveniently refer to them if questions about acceptable behavior or procedures, including age restrictions, arise.

In general, signage is not an effective means to communicate detailed information.

> No amount of signs or shushing, rules or intervention can possi-
> bly be as effective as building the skills, knowledge and attitudes
> of library workers to meet young adults where they are at—and
> to help them find the solutions, a sense of identity and the posi-
> tive interactions they need to avoid risky behaviours and to grow
> into resilient adults. (Mylee 2010)

Just as it's impossible to try to devise a rule for every situation, it's impossible to post a sign that tries to list every infraction or possible exception (in spectacular detail).

Signs don't work as a means to communicate rules. People don't read signs—they are white noise in a cluttered landscape of visual information. The type of impression signs can make on teen users is negative and hostile (intentionally or not). Librarians should consider their own reactions to posted rules and how signs can create an unwelcoming atmosphere in places like stores and government offices. This is the opposite of the service ambience a library should project.

Teen services librarians should strive to create connections. When working with teens, every interaction is an opportunity to foster a relationship with the library; this includes occasions when staff can help teens understand and navigate library rules. Teen services librarians need to be customer-focused and hands-on. Even in the midst of an infraction, a librarian should take the time to talk to teen patrons about the library's behavioral expectations: what is and is not okay in the library setting, and most importantly, why. A sign can't do that—only a person can, because:

- Signs aren't a substitute for staff taking initiative to mitigate problems as they arise with teen users (even if the staff finds this repetitive).
- Pointing to a sign does not take the place of interacting with teen users in any service situation.
- The presence of a sign does not impart an understanding of the rules.

Application of Rules by Library Staff

TEEN BEHAVIOR: TAKE NOTHING FOR GRANTED

Teens aren't born knowing how to use the library. A trip to the library might be a teen's first independent excursion to a public place. This initial autonomy may manifest as rambunctious exuberance or self-conscious quietness. Not every teen (or child or adult) who walks through the library door understands behavioral expectations for public places— including the library. If librarians expect that teens have the life experience and knowledge to act appropriately in all situations, these expectations can lead to misunderstandings and trouble. As advocates for teens in the organization, part of the teen services librarian's role is to help teens navigate the library landscape; this goes beyond the librarian's skill at readers' advisory, or knowledge of the YA fiction collection. This has to do with the day-to-day realities of working with teens in the library setting, developing a rapport with teen library users, and establishing a short list of techniques to be used in service situations.

Every librarian will experience situations where the behavior of patrons, including teens, is disruptive or violates an established patron code of conduct. Librarians must mediate these situations to assure the safe enjoyment of the library by all users. How often disruptions occur and how successfully they are mediated depends upon the unique dynamics of a given library and the capacity of its staff to communicate with users.

Staff's automatic impulse for every infraction may be to throw teens out. This may seem like an effective short-term solution, but it does not address any underlying problems that may precipitate negative situations. Rather than throwing teens out, staff should seize this opportunity to help teens understand what the accepted norms are. This has the added benefit of helping staff with their expectations that a given teen or group of teens is equipped with the understanding of what is and isn't okay to do in the library. Often teens simply don't realize that they're breaking a rule until they've been verbally informed of its existence (Harden and Huggins 2004) or asked to leave (which can be expedient but shouldn't be a first or second resort).

The goal should be to avoid problems before they occur, and when they do occur, to resolve situations without escalating them. Rules should be crafted and applied consistently, and staff members should deal with problem behavior in real time.

If staff find themselves repeatedly calling security or asking teens to leave the library, the manner in which they mitigate teen behavior must be examined. The end goal is that security should seldom be called to deal with teen behavior, teens are not regularly asked to leave, and teens are rarely "banned" from the library.

The only behavioral element that truly is in the library's control is the conduct of staff—not of patrons. The behavior of patrons is something that the library attempts to manage through policy, rules, and the capacity of staff to mediate challenging situations with the public. This capacity can be improved with simple techniques, including the use of a progressive approach for managing problem behaviors that is consistently applied by all staff members. As staff recognizes the role it plays in mitigating teen behavioral issues, incidents should decrease and service to teens improve.

CONSISTENCY

Teens are keenly aware of fairness. Library staff should enforce library policy and rules consistently and respectfully while separating annoying behaviors from disorderly and possibly criminal behaviors and acting accordingly (Brehm-Heeger 2008). Library staff must enforce rules and impose consequences consistently without over- or underreacting.

Some staff members may underreact. They may ignore misbehavior because of apathy, laziness, or fear of confrontation. Underreaction can also include letting teens slide and not taking appropriate steps in the face of obvious infractions. This might be because the staff member is fond of a particular teen, does not want to be perceived as a mean person, or wants to be liked.

Overreacting is as bad as underreacting. If every infraction is punishable by expulsion, then teens may consider going big and then going home. (If you get a life sentence for stealing candy or for stealing a car—then go for the car. The consequences are the same.) If teens are laughing too loudly—they get thrown out. If teens fight—they get thrown out. Teens who are conditioned by this dynamic may cultivate an "If I'm going to get thrown out anyway . . ." mentality.

Consequences for an infraction should be the same for all people. A large group has assembled in the library's lobby and is laughing and speaking in excited tones. The way staff react to this group will depend on the type of people who make up the group. Although staff may react differently to a large group of senior citizens from the local genealogy club, a group of toddlers happy and excited after story time, or a group of teens headed toward the teen space during the after-school rush, they must treat each group the same way. There cannot be different standards of behavior for different groups. Teen services librarians must be prepared to point out if rules are applied inconsistently.

Teens quickly notice if rules only apply at certain times for certain people and with certain staff members. If the rules are always changing, then there really aren't any rules. Inconsistency invites chaos. Because of the power structure, teens often bear the brunt of the rules that staff apply inconsistently. They may pay the penalty for the actions of adults.

INCONSISTENCY BUILDS UP

The after-school rush can be used as an example of how inconsistently applying rules reinforces and even encourages inappropriate behavior in teens. Some libraries experience a phenomenon where the "bad behavior" of teens seemingly escalates during the course of the school year; by late in the school year teens are seemingly out of control and staff find themselves dealing with infractions that have been festering for months. Because some staff members have been more permissive than others, and rules and consequences were employed arbitrarily, teens have learned that there is no sense of fairness. Staff have demonstrated that there really are no rules and no one is really in charge. Things have gone all *Lord of the Flies.* Although staff may believe they are dealing with the misbehavior of individual teens, they are in fact dealing with the consequences of a group dynamic that they have created. Toward the end of a semester of inconsistent enforcement, library staff is primed to vigorously apply rules during the after-school rush.

At the beginning of every school year, the teen services librarian should review procedures for dealing with problem behavior with colleagues, and remind them that staff conduct is the catalyst for conflict. Dealing with problem behaviors as they occur isn't optional—it's a job requirement.

Real-World Tactics: Managing Problem Behavior

When faced with inappropriate behavior it can be tricky to know what to do. The way these situations are managed by staff can extinguish or escalate the problem.

As advocates for teens, teen services librarians must be vigilant about identifying and addressing instances where staff inconsistently apply rules to teen patrons or when teens are subject to different rules or standards than other library patron groups. Consistently applying rules isn't a customer service issue—it is an ethical issue.

> Consistency of staff response is essential to ethical rule enforcement. As in the provision of service, whether and how a rule is enforced should not depend either on the identity of the staff

member in charge or the identity of the patron whose conduct is
the issue. (Preer 2008)

It is vital to employ a consistent strategy when dealing with problem
behavior. Teens are acutely aware of fairness, and the strategy proposed
below places choices about and responsibility for actions squarely on
them. Staff informs teens about specific problems, which gives them the
opportunity to do something positive by complying with staff's request
that they modify their behavior. Ideally, the strategy will help teens
understand behavioral expectations and counteract staff assumptions
that teens already know what is acceptable, which should ultimately
result in an improvement of the teen/librarian relationship.

> **Be firm but kind.** Often the presence of the teen services librarian or
> another staff member is enough to curb unwanted behavior (when
> the teen is aware that the behavior is unwanted). A staff mem-
> ber stomping over to a table full of noisy teens is a setup for con-
> flict. Keeping a calm, neutral demeanor is important. Walking over
> while smiling and saying, "Hi, guys" sets the tone for the exchange
> (and may disarm teens prepared to be defensive). Teens are accus-
> tomed to being yelled at and told what to do by adults. It is vital
> that the teen services librarian (and any library staff members) do
> not contribute to this dynamic. Teen services librarians and staff
> members working with teens must be aware of how they speak to
> them. Whatever their individual service style, staff members must
> maintain a professional tone and demeanor,

> **Be clear about what the issue is.** Any explanation of the situation
> must be clear and concise. Telling a teen to "start behaving" is
> ambiguous. If the problem is that the teen is yelling, the teen ser-
> vices librarian should name the specific problematic behavior.

> **Ask for a favor.** When a problem behavior occurs, asking "Would
> you do me a favor?" is a way to request that a teen change her
> behavior that places all the power with the teen. She has a choice:
> She can choose to modify her behavior or not. Staff can begin by
> naming the behavior and then making a request: "You are yelling.
> Would you do me a favor and speak more quietly?" This language

is positive. The request is positive. It highlights what the teen could do, rather than what the teen should stop doing. The teen isn't lectured and no rules are invoked.

If the teen complies, the librarian should thank her at an appropriate moment (e.g., when she is leaving or when the librarian is going off desk). A simple "thanks for helping me out today" will do. There is no need to make a speech about how nice it was that she quieted down after being asked, and how it is important not to be noisy.

If the teen does not comply, when the librarian has already informed the teen of the problem and asked for a favor, then it's time to let the teen know what the consequences are for further noncompliance.

If the teen does not comply, then offer a choice. Say "I asked you to quiet down and you've chosen not to. If you choose to continue talking so loudly I'll have to ask you leave for the rest of the day."

If the teen does not comply after a choice is offered, then it's time to employ the established consequences.

Employ consequences. Say "I've asked you twice to please quiet down and you've chosen not to. I told you that if you chose not to you would have to leave for the rest of the day. Because you've decided not to speak more quietly, you are going to have to leave for the rest of the day."

Invite the teen to return. Say "I hope I see you tomorrow."

Keep things simple and about now. Keep the focus on behaviors—not people or personalities. The current situation doesn't have anything to do with what happened with the same teen yesterday—or three months ago. It is about what is happening now. Informing the teen of the specific problem gives her the opportunity to do something good (e.g., a favor) by complying.

Return after suspension. If a teen has been asked to leave and not come back for a day, for example, the manner in which his return to the library is handled is crucial and sets an important tone.

Every day is a new day after the teen returns to the library. This is not an opportunity to lecture, rehash what happened, or to issue further warnings. This is a chance to welcome the teen back and give some positive reinforcement. This welcoming attitude will allay any fears the teen may have of returning to the library and will show that the librarian was true to the promise that the one-day expulsion was just that—one day. "I really like that you come to the library and I'm glad that you are back. If you have any questions about what's okay to do and what's not okay to do you can always ask me. Okay?"

Using these methods takes the "bad guy" out of what the librarian is doing, and lets the teen make all the decisions. The librarian objectively describes the choices the teen has made and the consequences of her actions.

The librarian should never express anger (even if she is angry!). A negative response from the librarian might be the type of attention that the teen expects or desires. The adult staff member has to be, well, the adult. Even if the teen curses or calls the librarian names, the librarian must maintain a professional, neutral demeanor.

If something happens that must be dealt with swiftly, but doesn't lend itself to the favor/choices/consequences/invitation sequence discussed above, the suspension can be given the next time the teen visits the library. He should be told that because of what happened he will not be able to return to the library for a certain period of time (e.g., three days or a week).

If a teen is told not to visit the library again for an extended period, the best practice is to tell the teen that when he returns he must speak to a staff person (e.g., the teen services librarian or a manager) before he can use the library. The date after which he may return and the name and phone number of the staff person he must speak to is written down and given to the teen. As with any patron suspension, staff should be informed of the date the teen can return, and about the conversation that must take place.

The conversation that takes place when the teen returns is an opportunity for staff to welcome the teen back to the library, and to assure him that the library is glad he's back. This is not the time to relitigate why the teen was asked to leave in the first place, nor is it the time to give a lecture or make preemptive threats. It's important to ask the teen if he has any questions about the situation or its consequences. This is a good time to tell the teen that if he ever has any questions about what is or isn't okay in the library, has any questions or concerns about the library, or feels he is being mistreated, he should come and talk to the librarian.

Sometimes incidents of repeated rule-breaking cannot be remedied with the technique outlined above. No matter how well staff articulates choices and consequences, there will be occasions when some teens (like some adults) choose not to comply. Teens don't leave their lives at the door—and neither do we (Terrile and Echols 2012).

WHERE DO PARENTS FIT?

Navigating rules and testing limits are normal teen behaviors. The library should be a place where this can occur. Avoid calling parents in cases where rules have been broken or suspensions from the library have been issued. The librarian should handle problem behavior in a way that maintains the privacy of the teen.

If a teen's behavior is serious enough to warrant a parent being notified, it should only be in situations where law enforcement is involved, and a representative of the law enforcement agency should be responsible for contacting a parent.

WHEN SHOULD POLICE BE CALLED?

Librarians should understand the difference between an infraction of the patron code of conduct and the violation of a law. Call the police if a law is broken or if staff or patrons are in danger. Security expert Steven Albrecht suggests that librarians listen to their guts when it comes to calling the police. If you think you should call the police, then call them (Pera 2014).

Albrecht reminds librarians that although the presence of a police officer has a calming effect on situations, staff should use common sense before contacting local authorities. Calling police officers to deal with minor infractions of the library's code of conduct is akin to crying wolf. Involving the police in minor code infractions may also anger parents who consider it an overreaction to behavior that is not criminal.

SOAPBOX MOMENT

Now, Say That in Front of His Mother

To ensure you always treat a teen respectfully, here's a rule of thumb: Never say anything to a teen that you would not say to her in front of her mother. It's a handy trick that will help keep your temper in check. and moderate the tone and content of any admonitions you make to teens. Remember, you are the adult in the situation. Run it through this filter to be sure you'd say that same thing in the same way in front of her mother.

REFERENCES

Brehm-Heeger, Paula. 2008. *Serving Urban Teens.* Westport: CT: Libraries Unlimited.

Chelton, Mary K. 2002. "The 'Problem Patron' Public Libraries Created," *The Reference Librarian,* 36 (75): 23–32.

Jones, Patrick, and Joel Shoemaker. 2001. *Do It Right! Best Practices for Serving Young Adults in School and Public Libraries.* New York: Neal-Schuman Publishers.

Harden, Susan B., and Melanie Huggins. 2004. "Here Comes Trouble: A Surefire Approach that Works with Unruly Teens." *School Library Journal* 50 (7): 32–35.

Mylee, Joseph. 2010. "An Exquisite Paradox: Making Teens and Young Adults Welcome in Public Libraries." *Australasian Public Libraries and Information Services* 23 (3).

Pera, Mariam. 2014. "AL Live: Library Security." *The Scoop* (blog). May 14. http://americanlibrariesmagazine.org/blog/al-live-library-security.

Preer, Jean L., 2008. *Library Ethics.* Westport, CT: Libraries Unlimited.

Terrile, Vikki C., and S. Michele Echols. 2012. "They Don't Leave Their Lives at the Door, But Neither Do We: Changing Our Minds about Changing Teens' Behaviors." *Young Adult Library Services* 10 (2): 19–23.

5

ACCESS, CONTROL, AND PRIVACY

KEY CONSIDERATIONS

- Is there ever an appropriate circumstance when a parent or guardian should be called about a teen's behavior in the library? What agency should initiate this call?
- What responsibility does the library have regarding suspected truant teens?
- What expectations should teens have while using the library? Should these expectations be different than those of adults?
- Is it ever appropriate for the library to require teens to engage in certain activities?

Day-to-Day Living

Teen services librarians may often be put in the position of mediating situations that occur between parents and their teen-age children, such as questions about the teen's whereabouts or her activities while visiting the library. They may also find themselves in situations where information volunteered by a teen is of a nature so serious that it must be reported to authorities.

Being able to tell these situations apart, and understanding the limitations and responsibilities of the public library, is vital to navigating circumstances that undoubtedly will arise while working with the public.

It may be easier to determine what to do in a drastic situation than how to deal with some of the nuanced situations that arise when interacting with teens (or any members of the public, for that matter) in the public library setting. If the library is on fire, the parameters of what actions to take are pretty obvious. As Anton Chekov said in *The Cherry Orchard* (1904), "any idiot can handle a crisis; it's [the] day-to-day living that wears you out."

The vast array of challenging situations staff must mediate on a day-to-day basis and the variety of possible responses to these situations can cause confusion and create inconsistency in how certain circumstances are addressed in the library. They can also wear staff down.

In contrast to the behavioral expectations for patrons articulated by the library (how the library expects users to act) there are issues that deal with access and control imposed upon users by the library (how the library acts toward users, via limitations, requirement, and procedures) and these limitations have teen patron privacy implications.

Librarians are familiar with the concepts of access and control, but tend to view them narrowly: they may consider access only in terms of censorship and availability of resources, and control solely as it relates to patron behavior and codes of conduct. But the thread of privacy runs through both access and control. A myopic view of access and control can cause libraries to overlook possible violations of the privacy of teen users.

Teen services librarians must be aware that, within their organizations, teens may be subject to different processes than other patron populations regarding privacy while using the library facility, including access to the library as a whole or particular areas of the library space, and restricted or required activities other patron populations are not subjected to.

Open Access

Teens should never have to explain why they are in the library. Libraries have articulated policies on privacy and access that are focused on borrowing habits, patron records, and the right to read. The American Library Association's "Library Bill of Rights" addresses access issues that go beyond policy and that speak to the totality of library services

(ALA 1996). When teens are restricted from using the library simply because they are teens, or if they must explain why they want to use the library, the library is not following the guidelines of the American Library Association.

Article Five of the "Library Bill of Rights" states: "A person's right to use a library should not be denied or abridged because of origin, age, background, or views" (ALA 1996). Period. Further, "Free Access to Libraries for Minors: An Interpretation of the Library Bill of Rights" states:

> Library policies and procedures that effectively deny minors equal and equitable access to all library resources available to other users violate the Library Bill of Rights. The American Library Association opposes all attempts to restrict access to library services, materials, and facilities based on the age of library users. (ALA 2004a)

ALA's "Freedom to Read" and "Freedom to View" statements (ALA 1989; ALA 2004b) state in no uncertain terms that it is the parents' responsibility to guide their minor children's choices about what is appropriate to read. The library doesn't make those decisions for teens (and every librarian should cringe at the thought of asking a teen why they want a particular book), or telling a teen that a book on a particular subject is not appropriate for them. Librarians must understand that open access to information is a core value.

Similarly, every librarian should understand that all of the following are also equal abridgements of the teen's right to use the library:

- asking teens why they are present in the library or if they should be somewhere else (e.g., in school)
- denying or restricting the time of day when teens may enter the library or part of the library
- volunteering personal information about teens while they are in the library by paging or otherwise identifying them
- contacting schools to report suspected truancy
- reporting inappropriate behavior to parents or caregivers

Because librarians may focus on privacy as it relates to censorship and open access to material, it is not uncommon for libraries to impose restrictions that contradict the Library Bill of Rights when those restrictions are related to teens' physical access to all areas of the library or even the library itself. The library may be motivated by safety concerns, but teen services librarians should be vigilant when restrictions on access apply only to members of a single user group. Teen services librarians should strive to bring their organizations in line with ALA policy on equality of treatment and service for teen patrons.

REQUIRED ACTIVITIES / LIMITED ACTIVITIES

Provided teens are not causing disruptions, the activities they engage in while visiting the library are, frankly, nobody's business. Teens who choose to visit the library after school and sit around a table socializing are absolutely using the library in a legitimate, developmentally appropriate manner.

When a library requires teens to complete specific activities before they can use the library as they wish (e.g., by imposing one-hour of homework before allowing them to use computers for games or social networking), the library is infringing upon teens' freedom to enjoy the library.

This desire to guide and direct the activities of teens may come from a genuine concern for teens' well-being, but it contradicts the idea that teens should be able to pursue whatever activity they choose while visiting the library.

If three ladies pull out their knitting while chatting around a library table, staff wouldn't think twice about it. They wouldn't be required to participate in a sanctioned activity before engaging in a self-selected activity. Adults don't generally tell other adults what to do unless rules are broken. Similarly, it's unlikely that anyone would ask the ladies if they are supposed to be somewhere else.

In their conduct policies, some libraries try to define which activities are permitted by suggesting suitable uses of the library. For example, the general conduct policy of the Houston Public Library defines what the library is for: reading, studying, writing, using library materials, and participating in scheduled programs or meetings (Houston Public Library 2005). This positive definition states what *is* possible instead of what *is not.* But a definition lists specific activities may imply that these are the *only* activities appropriate in the library.

New York's Schenectady Public Library also uses a positive definition to state what patrons can do while visiting the library—patrons may "engage in activities associated with the use of a public library. Patrons who are not reading, studying, using library materials or attending events may be asked to leave the building" (www.scpl.org/about_us/policies.html). Rather than presenting a litany of what activities are not permitted, the policy enumerates what activities are allowed in the library. But this narrow definition may lead to confusion on the part of both public and staff. Librarians may interpret this rule to mean that any activity occurring outside of these narrow parameters is not allowed. Misinterpreting it might lead them to apply it differently to different user groups.

The use of positive definitions and restrictive language may suggest to librarians that they can limit what activities teens may engage in while visiting the library, even if they are not causing disturbances. If applied literally, narrow definitions of accepted activities contradict the idea of the library as a community gathering place: an agora, a hangout spot, a place to knit, a venue for fostering democracy and community. Limiting the activities that are deemed acceptable in the library will also limit the definition of the library itself.

Status Offenses and Time of Day Restrictions

A status offense is conduct that is unlawful because of the person's age. In other words, an adult may legally engage in the same act that is considered a status offense if it is performed by a minor (Kendall 2007). An example of a status offense is limiting who can consume alcohol—it's not illegal for an adult over the age of 21 to drink alcohol but it is for a minor under the age of 21. Truancy is also a status offense. If a person is over eighteen (i.e., an adult) he or she cannot be truant, nor can a person eighteen or older be in noncompliance with a daytime curfew that applies to minors.

Because both school and public libraries also serve children and teens, there can be a misperception that the public library functions the same way they do. The legal term *in loco parentis* literally translates from Latin as "in the place of a parent." It is a legal doctrine that describes a relationship where a person or entity assumes parental duties and obligations for another individual, usually a young person. Schools act in the place of parents, which is why schools have to feed students, make medical care available in the form of a school nurse, provide transportation to and from school, and enact dress codes (and in days gone by, employ corporal punishment).

Schools serve in loco parentis; public libraries do not.

Libraries should not call authorities to report suspected truants. Everyone can agree that the best place for a high school student to be during the school day is in school, but the responsibility for the whereabouts of students is squarely placed on the parents and schools via the doctrine of in loco parentis—the library is not required to deal with truancy.

Former corrections officer and truant officer turned librarian Sheila Bryant explains it this way:

> Essentially, public librarians are not *in loco parentis* [in the place of a parent] and have no duty to report suspected truancy . . . Please note that it is solely the parent's responsibility to comply with the compulsory education of their children and no one else. (Bryant 2006)

In other words, the public library is not responsible for children and teens missing school, but it is the parents' responsibility.

PAPERS PLEASE

Some libraries state in their policies that teens of school age present in the library during school hours will be asked for "proof" that they are visiting the library for a legitimate reason. Just by virtue of their presence in the library, teens—or adults who look as though they might be under eighteen—are subject to questioning by staff or security guards. Approaching a teen and asking if they should be in school:

- is an invasion of privacy based on age or appearance
- assumes that all teens are supposed to be in school, even though some may have dropped out or been expelled or suspended
- disregards non-traditional school options like homeschooling and alternative schooling

If a library agrees to police truancy, it can then be held responsible when they do not report it. This leaves the library open to liability. Library staff should not ask any patrons if they should be somewhere else (like work, jail, or visiting a probation office), but if a police officer wants to ask someone for her ID because the officer thinks the adult may have outstanding warrants, they are welcome to enter the library for that purpose.

Libraries should be cautious about accepting responsibility for truancy by writing it into policies regarding minors. The unattended children policy of the Winfield (Illinois) Public Library states that children ages six to sixteen are "free to utilize the library unattended as long as needed, provided their behavior is not disruptive to other patrons or library personnel. Exceptions to this are cases of suspected child neglect or truancy" (Winfield Library 2011). The policy defines truancy as the "attendance at the library of a school-age child during regular school hours," and outlines procedures for dealing with suspected truancy. The librarian is to ask the minor to show "evidence of a legitimate cause for absence from school." In the event that the librarian does not accept the cause for absence, the librarian will contact the school and the child's parents. If the child refuses to supply any evidence or identification, the police are to be contacted (Winfield Library 2011).

In a similar policy, Baltimore's Enoch Pratt Free Library also reserves the right to contact the authorities if children or teens are in the library on school days from 9:00 am to 3:00 pm without written proof from school authorities excusing them from school on that day (Enoch Pratt Free Library n.d.).

There are many points in such procedures where the librarian is called upon to make judgments on issues that are not related to the library. Any policy that obligates library staff to ask for information, determine the validity of proof, and contact authorities or parents is a violation of privacy and a huge responsibility to place upon the librarian and the library.

It is suggested that libraries articulate the limitations of their responsibility for school-age teens during school hours. For example, Ohio's Toledo-Lucas County Public Library has a clear policy regarding suspected truancy. It states simply that the Toledo-Lucas County Public

Library should not report suspected truancies, and that reporting truancies is the responsibility of parents, truant officers, and the police (Toledo-Lucas County Board of Trustees 2007).

HOMESCHOOLED TEENS, DROP-OUTS, AND NONTRADITIONAL STUDENTS

Limiting or restricting the hours teenagers can be in the library during the school day might give the impression that libraries do not value youth who are taking a nontraditional path in their schooling. A teen who has dropped out of high school, is homeschooled, or attends an alternative school cannot be truant—but they most certainly are teens. Teens who have dropped out of school certainly cannot furnish written proof from school authorities excusing them from school.

The library can be a good youth service community member by letting schools know that if they suspect their students are truant and in the library during school hours, a school is welcome to send school district police, vice principals, or truant officers to investigate, but that library staff will never initiate a call to the school if it appears that its students are present.

DAYTIME CURFEWS AND DE FACTO AGE RESTRICTIONS

Some libraries schedule the opening times of designated teen areas to align with after-school hours, so that these areas only need to be staffed during heavy traffic hours. The side effect of this is that it prohibits teens who use the library during school hours from using the teen space.

This can mean teens have limited access to the YA collection or the computers designated for their use. Making a separate teen space available only after school restricts services for teens that are homeschooled, that have left school without graduating—and, yes, those who are truant. This may also limit the access to the teen space by a school tour group—which wastes an invaluable opportunity to showcase the library's offerings to teens and to invite them back to the library to participate in program development and earn volunteer service hours for school.

Although this kill-two-birds-with-one-stone hours-of-operation strategy may be practical for libraries because of limited availability of teen services staff for the teen space, it's important to consider the consequences of limiting access to teen services and staff. The de facto outcome is that the library is closed to teens for part of the day, which is an abridgement of equal access.

Privacy, Safety, and Confidentiality

Librarians may automatically honor requests for information about the presence of teens in the library building without considering the privacy, safety, and confidentiality concerns inherent in such requests. Although most requests about the whereabouts of a particular teen are benign, some may not be. What is certain is that any disclosure about whether or not a teen has visited or is visiting the library, and what activities they have engaged in, is a violation of patron privacy equal to disclosing what books a teen has checked out. Librarians should also be wary of parents who ask them to monitor their teen-age children's activities during library visits. Any sensitive information teens share with librarians must remain confidential.

How much is appropriate to disclose can be complicated to understand in the day-to-day context of the library. Teen services librarians should familiarize themselves with the child protection policies in force for their municipalities, and abide by them. It is also important to follow the rules the library has set forth for dealing with situations that may arise. A regular examination of these procedures and policies is important to assure that all patrons are being treated equally and that the rights of teens to reasonable privacy and access while visiting the library are protected. Teen services librarians must know the policies, question the policies (as needed), and help to make the policies workable for everyone.

PUBLIC ADDRESS SYSTEM PAGING

In the age of mobile communication, the request to page a teen at the library might seem quaint. Paging, or using the public address system to summon an individual by name, is one example of how librarians may be asked to divulge the whereabouts of teen library users.

Paging might be an area where the library acts without considering possible violations of privacy inherent in the actions of staff. Paging anyone over the public address system in the library can be a violation of patron privacy. Regardless of communication options or platforms, at the heart of a paging request is the solicitation of information about the whereabouts of an individual (in this case if an individual is currently present in the library).

Libraries should have a policy in place regarding the use of the public address system. The San José Public Library's Public Address System policy leaves no room for ambiguity regarding paging customers. It states:

> The public address system in the King Library is used *only* for Library opening and closing announcements or for emergency instructions.
>
> There will be absolutely *no* paging of customers, announcement of programs, or other incidental uses of this system. (http://www.sjpl.org/policies-procedures/public-address-system-policy)

The Library Law blog addresses the topic of paging patrons as it relates to women being harassed by partners against whom they have restraining orders, but the essence of what the blog suggests is the same when applied to teens (Bryant 2006).

There is no way that the library can know what child custody or restraining orders might be in play in any given situation. Although it may seem extreme, it is suggested that libraries err on the side of caution, and stress that for the safety and security of teens the library does not offer information regarding the whereabouts of teens (or, for that matter, anyone) in the library.

The same rationale that prohibits paging teens applies to in-person inquiries, too. Even someone with a missing persons flier—unless it is a police officer—should not be given information about who has visited the library.

Answering questions about teens' whereabouts is a level of responsibility the library should not take on. The library is not responsible for knowing where minors are—that is a parent's job. The impulse might be to provide information to parents about whether or not their teen-age children are or were in the library. The following sample dialogues can serve as a conversation starter for professional development training where teen services librarians can introduce the treatment of these types of situations to colleagues and managers. This conversation is a good exercise to get everyone on staff on the same page about how to respond to these requests.

In person:

> **Adult.** Page my son, I can't find him.

> **Library staff.** We don't use the public address system to page people. You're welcome to walk through and look for him.

On the phone:

> **Adult.** Is my son there now?

> **Library staff.** We don't page people in the library. This is for everyone's safety and privacy. Respectfully, please understand that there is really no way for us to know who is calling and asking about where minors are. You are welcome to drop by the library to look for them.

> **Adult.** But this is an emergency.

> **Library staff.** You can have a family member or friend drop by the library—or call the police and have an officer come to the library to look for your son.

On the phone or in person:

> **Adult.** Can you tell me if my son was at the library yesterday?

> **Library staff.** I don't know.

Are there exceptions? Yes. Every situation is different and librarians must use their judgment and critical thinking skills. Many variables, from the size of the community to the presence of library security and extenuating circumstances will come into play. Consistency and common sense are key in these situations.

There is more art than science here, but the bottom line is that the library should not disclose information about who or when teens use the library. Reasonable accommodation should be made for emergencies based on individual circumstances.

FAMILY RULES

Librarians are familiar with having members of the public request the reconsideration of material the library has purchased. The library's collection development statement helps guide and defend how materials are selected. If a parent tells a librarian that she doesn't want her child to check out books on a certain subject, the librarian is most likely comfortable expressing that it is up to the parents to shape their own child's use of the library's collection. If the librarian is asked by a parent to monitor what the teen accesses through the library's technology (e.g., "I don't want my son going to [social media site] when he is on the library computer"), the librarian should be equally prepared to respond. The medium is different, but the talking points are the same as those used with resources.

The American Library Association's "Free Access to Libraries for Minors: An Interpretation of the Library Bill of Rights" states, "Librarians and governing bodies should maintain that *parents—and only parents*—have the right and the responsibility to restrict the access of their children—and only their children—to library resources" (ALA 2004).

Librarians cannot assume the role of parents or the functions of parental authority in the private relationship between parents and their minor children. Expressing this to a parent of a teen, as in the situation outlined about, can take the form of family rules. The teen services librarian can try any of these talking points:

> What's right for your child to read/view/access can only be decided and enforced by you. I certainly don't want anyone but me deciding what is appropriate for my child to read/view/access.

> Only you know what's appropriate for your child to read/view/access.

> I don't know what rules your family has, and it's between the members of the family to enforce and follow family rules.

> You are welcome to stay with your children and monitor their computer use.

It is not appropriate for library staff to offer to police a family's rule. This is not the library's responsibility—if the teen is not violating the library's code of conduct then the librarian shouldn't tell him anything about what he accesses, reads, or views in the library. So, if the teen decides to access a social media site that a parent has banned, it's a matter that is strictly between the parents and their child.

Real-World Tactics: Teen Confides Sensitive Information

It is normal and necessary for teen services librarians to form relationships with the teens in the service community. This involves hearing about the everyday ups-and-downs of teens' lives at home, at school, and with friends.

Librarians should be sure that they don't enter in to a pattern with teen regulars where they solicit adult attention by talking about their personal problems or challenges. Teens who are lonely or in need of positive attention from an adult may find that a sympathetic staff member listens to them talk about their problems. However, this may reinforce that the teen is getting attention only because of a crisis. If the situation does not involve abuse, neglect, or other illegal activities, the librarian should reinforce the constructive aspects of the teen's visit to the library. Placing the teen in charge of completing tasks to help the librarian (e.g., by decorating a bulletin board or helping straighten the shelves) is a way the teen's presence and participation can be acknowledged positively.

It is normal for teens to tell trusted librarians about situations they experience in day-to-day life. Librarians may hear about issues that exceed the purview of the reference interview or the capacity of the library organization, ranging from teens' fears that a teacher doesn't like them to worries about sexual health and abuse.

Eventually, every teen services librarian finds himself in a situation where a teen confides sensitive information or asks for assistance with a serious life situation in an arena where the library is unable to provide direct help. This may be a situation of abuse or neglect, substance abuse, homelessness, or unplanned pregnancy. Although the library cannot directly provide a place to sleep or legal assistance, it can provide information to help teens get the community services they need. Providing information is what librarians do best—we are connectors. If a teen has a problem, the librarian is uniquely positioned to find help, and to assist in the basic mediation of contact with appropriate agencies.

Offering assistance by contacting community agencies removes the librarian from directly providing a solution to a problem. This is accomplished by using the librarian's skills in providing nonjudgmental access to information. The librarian can furnish phone numbers and addresses to local agencies, provide a phone, or even ask the teen if they would like the librarian to initiate the call. That call might sound something like this:

> Hi. This is Jennifer at the library and I have a teen here that needs to get some information from you. Her name is Mary, she is fifteen years old. I'm passing the phone to her now . . .

Situations like these are difficult, and every teen services librarian will have heard, or will hear, stories she wished she never had. Remember that the best way to serve a teen in need is to do what librarians do best—connect teens with information important to their quality of life.

WHERE PRIVACY ENDS AND OBLIGATION BEGINS

Cherie Givens (2013) explores the doctrine of in loco parentis as it applies to access to information and the rights teens have to privacy related to their library account information. Givens contrasts the responsibilities of the public or academic library versus the school library, and states that K–12 school librarians assume some in loco parentis responsibilities (Givens 2013). She elaborates on these responsibilities:

> Schools have a legal duty to protect their students in a different way from public and academic libraries . . . there is a special duty to report potentially dangerous behavior to the school guidance counselor or principal. Educators have a legal duty to report students who may have been abused, appear suicidal or in any way appear to be at risk. (Carson 2007)

If abuse, neglect, or other illegal situations are present or suspected, authorities should be contacted using established library policies and appropriate protocols.

If a teen states that he is being abused, the teen services librarian should tell him:

> You told me something that is really serious—and I want you to know that because I'm an adult I have to let someone know what

That One Time I Lost It with a High School Principal

A teen skipping school at the public library had a medical emergency. The principal arrived and aggressively asked why I let students into the library during the school day and if the local news showed up they would be wondering about that, too. I told him I'd be asking why his students could just walk off his campus.

The argument was satisfying, but I realized it was my responsibility to make sure the school understood the library's policy and position on truancy reporting. A new principal arrived in the fall and I show up every new school year at her office with library card applications, the Library's Truancy Reporting Policy, and cookies. Cookies.

you've told me. I care about you—and the community cares about you—and there are people that can help you in this situation.

Following the library's protocol, the librarian may call the police, non-emergency services (311), or local child protective services. The ideal situation is to have the teen make the report himself. The librarian should mention this option and perhaps even offer to mediate the beginning of the call:

It's really important that this is reported. You can use the phone in the back office. I'll stay with you. I will place the call for you— and if you want, I can explain a little about what's going on, then give the phone to you.

The hope is that the teen makes the report of his own accord, which is better than the teen becoming upset that the librarian is going to make the call. This may drive the teen away from a much-needed community resource, and he may stop coming to the library. If the teen leaves the library without making contact with authorities, the librarian is still obligated to report and should speak to a manager about protocols for the situation.

Teens aren't yet adults nor are they children, so the library often walks a tenuous line with how it treats teen users. An Unattended Child Policy may be a weird fit when applied to a minor child of sixteen. Policies that clearly state the limitations of the library's responsibilities for minors are important tools when dealing with parents, school officials, law enforcement, concerned citizens, and well-meaning coworkers.

REFERENCES

American Library Association. 1996. "Library Bill of Rights." Chicago: American Library Association. www.ala.org/advocacy/intfreedom/ librarybill.

———. 1989. "Freedom to View Statement." Chicago: American Library Association. www.ala.org/vrt/professionalresources/vrtresources/ freedomtoview.

———. 2004a. "Free Access to Libraries for Minors: An Interpretation of the Library Bill of Rights." Chicago: American Library Association. www.ala.org/Template.cfm?Section = interpretations&Template = / ContentManagement/ContentDisplay.cfm&ContentID = 8639.

———. 2004b. "Freedom to Read Statement." Chicago: American Library Association. www.ala.org/advocacy/intfreedom/statementspols/ freedomreadstatement.

Bryant, Sheila. 2006. *Truant Kids in the Library.* LibraryLaw Blog. http://blog .librarylaw.com/librarylaw/2006/03/truant_kids_in_.html.

Carson, Brian. 2007. *The Law of Libraries and Archives.* Lanham, MD: Scarecrow Press.

Enoch Pratt Free Library. *Unattended Children Policy.* www.prattlibrary.org/ about/index.aspx?id = 67472.

Givens, Cherie. 2013. "Intellectual Freedom or Protection? Conflicting Young Adults' Rights in Libraries." In *Transforming Young Adult Service.* Edited by Anthony Bernier. Chicago: Neal-Schuman Publishers.

Houston Public Library. 2005. *Rules and Policies.* www.houstonlibrary.org/ rules-and-policies.

Kendall, Jessica R. 2007. *Juvenile Status Offenses: Treatment and Early Intervention.* Edited by Catherine Hawke. American Bar Association. Division for Public Education.

San José Public Library. *Policies and Procedures: Public Address System Policy.* www.sjpl.org/policies-procedures/public-address-system-policy.

Schenectady Public Library Policies. *Appropriate Library Behavior.* www.scpl .org/about_us/policies.html.

Toledo-Lucas County Public Library. 2013. *Truancy Reporting Policies.* www .toledolibrary.org/pageselector.aspx?18021.

Winfield Public Library. 2011. *Unsupervised Children in the Library Policy.* www.winfield.lib.il.us/winfield/Policies/UnsupervisedChildren.pdf.

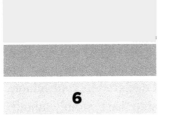

6

LIGHTNING ROUND
ADDRESSING COMMON ISSUES
AND CONCERNS

Questions may arise when considering how to apply the strategies suggested in this book. Although the situation and conditions at each library are unique, there are some concerns and situations that are universal.

Here, eleven specific teen services issues or concerns are proposed and discussed. Although it certainly isn't an exhaustive list, it includes issues that commonly arise in conversation when teen services librarians gather in formal and informal settings. The first three are addressed by teen services professionals Violeta Garza (Portland, Oregon), Carrie Kitchen (Calgary, Alberta, Canada), and Deborah Takahashi (Pasadena, California).

1. You Are Only Comfortable Working with Teens Who Are Similar to You.

by Violeta Garza

Do you find it difficult to work with teens that aren't like you (in terms of size, color, ethnicity, language preference, or lifestyle choices)?

Yes, working with talented and lovely teens who could be your MiniMe can be an absolutely delicious experience. They remind you of the best parts of yourself when you were a teen, you connect easily, and you can see yourself making an impact in their lives. "Sign me up!" anyone would say. "Being a librarian is amazing!" you would announce, and wait for a parade to be declared in your honor.

However, librarianship isn't simply about interacting with those teens who are already on a spectacular path to success, or those who are comfortable enough talking with adults that are like them. When working with teens you don't identify with, or when meeting that superstar author who touches your soul, or when encountering that good-looking and wonderfully irreverent actor or actress you currently have a crush on, these tips will help you be cool, accessible, and receptive.

Remind yourself that people are people

R.E.M.'s 1992 touchstone song and corresponding video taught us that, yes, everybody hurts, and everyone is human even when you think they aren't. Even the most confrontational teens care about someone. Even the most self-assured teens doubt themselves. Even the neediest teens give something positive of themselves to others. Even the most nonchalant teens want to be loved. In other words, while it may seem that you and youth live in different worlds, these worlds don't clash as much as you may expect.

Desensitize yourself to the differences, at least until you make a connection

Whether you're dealing with a Russian-speaking teen or a Somali refugee, don't dwell on what you think their lives are like. Don't assume that you know all about their relationships and home life based on stereotypes. Yes, stereotypes can prove to be truthful, but oftentimes they paint too simplistic a picture. Your teens are complex! They are more than their culture and their language.

Visualize the big picture that is a teen's entire life

Unless there was some strange Benjamin Button business going on, all teens were once babies. Their lives, often times filled with elements that are beyond their control, have influenced who they are. Yet all teens have been vulnerable. They have all felt embarrassed, or cried themselves to sleep, or wondered how the hell they're going to get through their situations. Think of the hottest teenage celebrities right now, and yes, they have also seen their lives go out of control. Life is life, and it touches everyone differently. In the end, though, teens are human, no matter what they look like, what they do with their free time, who they choose to love, and how they portray themselves to adults in the library.

Start with small, positive interactions and build from there

Those teens who are so different from you? They are likely accustomed to not having adults wade through difficulty to get to know them. Yet when you make the choice to interact—even if it's just to say hi—you make yourself a positive force. The real work begins when you make a connection with a teen who grew up speaking a different language than you, or has a different skin tone than you, or has a different lifestyle than you. Trying to assimilate them to your experience is not the goal, nor is having them tell you everything about their life stories. Simply being a non-judgmental adult in their lives can be helpful, especially if you acknowledge them when they are doing nothing wrong.

Search for common ground

It's impossible to find a human being who is the complete opposite of you. If you try to find similarities, you will find them. So search! All librarians are different, and so are teens. Honestly, you may be working with those teens who love to volunteer for the library, read like the apocalypse is just a day away, and joke around with adults. If you have these types of teens at your library, that's incredible! What you're seeing is a good phase. Everyone goes through ups and downs, even those overachieving teens who seem to have it all together. Most of the time, you will also be surrounded by teens who prefer to be on the computer, or who have no mental filter, or those who are so deadpan when you talk to them that you will not be able to get a reaction from them at all. And that's okay. They're people too.

2. You Are an Army of One, the Only Teen Services Librarian in the Library System.

by Carrie Kitchen

Picture this: a sprawling city of 1.2 million people, eighteen community libraries, roughly 120,000 teenagers—and one teen services librarian. That's my situation, as the only librarian devoted to teen services at Calgary Public Library in Calgary, Alberta, Canada. As you can imagine, it's a big job, and one that comes with its own set of challenges and opportunities.

Let me start with the opportunities: this is a position where the work I do makes a genuine difference, to teens and library staff throughout the city. From the start, I have had tremendous support from my managers and the rest of the team in the Services for Children, Teens, and Families (SCTF) department. As the system's expert on teen services, I have the chance to shape the direction of those services, and work on the areas that I think will have the biggest impact; that is a real privilege and a responsibility that I take very seriously.

When I was applying for this job, I had a candid conversation with the librarian who was leaving, and she told me that one of her biggest challenges had been feeling like she was on her own. This is something we often hear about as a challenge for solo librarians in small systems, but when you're the only person officially dedicated to an area, it's possible to feel isolated even in a large system. There may be times when it feels as though no one else cares about your passion, or shares your vision. So how do you turn this challenge into an opportunity? Easy— you create your own community. In a large system this means two networks; one external—created by joining YALSA, and connecting with teen librarians in other systems—and one internal, composed of other librarians and staff at all levels in your organization.

This doesn't have to be complicated; I started by creating a simple mailing list for any library staff who had an interest in YA lit or teen programming. That gave me an easy way to distribute information that needed to get out, and it helped those people find and connect with each other as well as with me. It also means that I have never felt alone— because although I am the only one with a job title devoted to teen services, I'm far from the only staff member who works with teens. Be available to everyone, and make sure they know it. I consider myself a point of contact for all of those staff members, and a big part of my job is encouraging each of them to work on teen services in their own locations; I support their work and make sure I share great ideas throughout the library system, so that we can all learn from each other, and so that none of us needs to feel like we're doing this alone.

Limited resources are another challenge, although hardly a unique one. A large urban library system has more resources, but also has to spread them across a larger area. Currently, we have no separate budget for teen services. The branches decide how to split their small programming budget between teens and children. In that environment, my task has become one of building capacity and maximizing resources across the system. I can't realistically ask a library to spend half of their budget on teen programming, but I can make that programming inexpensive and easy for their staff to host. For example, I developed a number of Youth Activity Kits, which provide supplies and instructions so that branches can host teen programs at virtually no cost and with very minimal staff time.

Staff training is an essential part of building capacity; not only will trained staff members be more comfortable and effective in serving teens, they will also become advocates for teen services at their locations (and, in my dreams at least, dedicated staff for my imaginary future teen services department). Training can be expensive, so work within the systems you have. This fall I will be teaching a new training module specifically on teen library services, but before that, I shoehorned what I consider crucial information about teen development and the 40 Developmental Assets into our existing readers' advisory training. I have gone to branch staff meetings to give quick Intro to Teen Services presentations, and visited branches to work with new librarians—I help with their weeding while I give them an orientation to their YA collections. There won't always be time or resources for formal training, but you can work teen services into quite a lot of conversations. Work on the foundations. By building capacity and awareness, and creating a framework for teen services at Calgary Public Library, I am making it easier for others to take on this work.

Finally, one of the greatest challenges in this position is feeling overwhelmed. Trust me—you are going to have moments, maybe lots of them, when you feel like you should be doing more: more programs, more outreach, more community connections, more advocacy, more copies of the hot new YA novel. I'm sure that's true for every librarian, but I feel it especially strongly knowing that I'm the only one who is doing this work; I'm the only teen services librarian, so if I'm not doing it, it isn't happening.

How do you avoid burnout? First, I have to realize that if I've done my job well, other staff members are starting to care about and work on teen services, so there are other people to catch the ball if I drop it. Second, never stop reaching for more, but understand that you are only one person and you can't do everything. Be aware of your limitations, choose your battles wisely, and accept that you will have to let some things go. I certainly don't mean that you should give up on doing your work well, just that you have to choose your priorities. My focus is on the library system as a whole, so if dropping one program at the Central Library gives me time to develop a kit that the whole system can use, that's the choice that I will make. It can be hard to decide what to let go of, but you won't be doing yourself or your teens any favors by getting so tired and frustrated that you end up quitting altogether.

Finally, just let yourself appreciate the rewards once in a while. Spend some time really looking at the results of your teen art contest, or having a conversation with a teen about great books or bands or movies they love. Take a deep breath, and remember why you chose teen services in the first place—it may have many challenges, but those are more than equaled by the rewards.

3. You Try to Relate to Teens in a "Cool Way," Often Using Teen Lingo. You Sense It Is Tragic. You Might Be Right.

by Deborah Takahashi

ON BEING GENUINE AND BEING YOURSELF

Attack with Kindness

Not only is it essential that we keep it real when working with teens, it is just as important to maintain who we are, let loose, and have fun. Teens literally have this sixth sense that allows them to gauge people. Depending on how we represent ourselves, this could lead to something great or blow up in our faces. For example, if we are closed off and quiet, then teens don't find us approachable. If we are nervous and afraid, they will sense this and take advantage of the situation. If we open ourselves up and attack with all of the kindness and joy that we have, we will scare the daylights out of them, but at least we have their attention. In my case, I do the latter and it has helped me do some amazing things. As teen librarians, we all have different personalities and quirks, so it's important that we embrace these qualities when interacting with teenagers; by showing them we are comfortable in our own skin it will break down some of the walls and clear a path for an actual dialogue. When we greet teens, we need to have the gumption to put ourselves out there and tell them that if they have questions about the collection or services, we are always there to help. Also, when they come to sit and hang out in the teen area, make it a point to get up from the desk and mingle in order to find common ground. Although we will have plenty of opportunities to show them we are down with their lingo and ways, it's best that we do that sparingly, otherwise, teens will be turned off. As teen librarians, the last thing we want to do is weird them out, because we are here to advocate for them—not to become that friend who constantly annoys them. More importantly, when teens approach us with serious questions, we need to have the flexibility and the willingness to switch gears to help them the best we can without feeling embarrassed or intimidated.

Listen

If there is one piece of advice I can give, it is to hone our listening skills. Teens really do appreciate it when we listen, because they tend to solve their issues as they actually discuss the problems. In other words, we end up becoming a soundboard, which is okay because it will help us hear what teens are struggling with emotionally, scholastically, and mentally. On the other hand, when they seek advice, try to be as honest as possible, but maintain a level of professionalism because we must be able to draw a line when the conversation gets iffy. Most of the time, the issues being discussed are fairly trivial and easily solved, but in some instances they can get personal or borderline inappropriate. If that is the case, we need to remind teens that certain topics are not appropriate to talk about with an adult, and end the conversation or change the topic. Teens definitely need reminding that we are not their friends, but their mentors and elders, and should be treated accordingly. As we continue to build relationships with teens, we need to be prepared for all types of scenarios that will require strength, courage, patience, and research. For example, if we somehow wind up in a conversation filled with acronyms, anime, and celebrity gossip, get ready to google #YOLO, check out Crunchyroll.com, and take mental notes of who is dating whom, and who is feuding with whom. Although this can be exhausting, we must also realize that all of the hours of reading, watching, listening, and learning are worth it, because it brings us that much closer to connecting with our teens, which is the most rewarding aspect of these relationships.

As we continue to talk with teens, we can actually ask them what they want from the library. When teens see that they can benefit from the library, they will realize that the library is actually listening to their suggestions and making changes to suit their needs. In fact, I was able to build a stellar manga collection with the help of the teen anime club. Teens who graduated high school two years ago always stop by to tell me how much they miss our conversations, and wished they had similar programs for people their age. By setting this kind of precedent, not only will we see a change in how we provide services, but we'll help build and inspire innovative and exciting programs that will help teens transition into the adult world. In many respects, the teen-librarian relationship is symbiotic because teen librarians are lost without input from teens, and vice versa. It really is amazing to see how little conversations can turn into viable products that will not only help teens, but remind us of why we do what we do. Finally, the really awesome part of forging these relationships is that we are actually making a difference in their lives. I joke constantly that they will forget about me in college, but, as I have learned, I am not easily forgotten because somehow, in some way, I have done something worth remembering. This is what being a teen librarian is about.

4. You Know More about Teen Authors than Teens. You Keep Talking about Reading and How Great YA Books Are Because You Want to Share the Joy of Reading—But These Teens Just Don't Care.

What happens in the library is about teens who are readers—and teens who are not. This is about making connections that foster a relationship with teens, information, and the library. Teens who are readers are going to read—and while reading is important and strongly associated with the traditions of the library, it is not the only activity teens can engage in at the library. Our job is not to proselytize and convert teens into readers. Our job is to facilitate the relationship teens want to have with the library, whatever form that takes.

Having resources within arm's length is beneficial to help teens make connections with subjects, but books and readers' advisory are not all the library has to offer. Just as new literacies are taking on new dimensions, so do the connections and relationships teens have with information. The move toward teens as curators and creators of content means shifting emphasis from librarian as expert guide to teens as full participants and decision-makers in their library experience. This involves connecting with bookworms in new and different ways.

The teen who loves to read and talk about books with you while you are on desk is a prime candidate for writing book reviews (peer-to-peer recommendation of resources), or using the library as a venue for her friends, whether or not they are readers.

During the course of my career I can count on one hand the number of times I've been involved with a teen book club—and the idea always came from teens. Two young women walked up to the desk and in the course of watching me place holds on books for them, they asked, "Do y'all have a book club for teens here?" My response was, "We do now. . . . And you're in charge." These endeavors lasted for only as long as the teens were enthusiastic about them, so they did not become crumbling edifices. In this case, the teens sustained the book club for several months during the school year, then it fell apart in the summer and never came back together. This illustrates how programming, and in particular teen-originated programming, is a living thing dependent on the needs and desires of teen originators.

5. You Have to Plan Teen Programs Six Months in Advance and Wonder How You Can Use the "Teen Participation" Model of Program Planning.

If this form of in-advance planning is a dictate from the PR department, it's important that the method of program "origination" be explained to them. What is important is that there is a growing and thriving teen programming effort, not a uniform and standardized calendar. What is more important, the dictates of the PR department or the efforts to build thriving teen participation in library programming efforts? The PR department is there to bring awareness to library services, not to direct, dictate, or involve itself in the development of library services and programming.

Consistency in programming is key. I can't remember when the third Thursday of the month is—why would I expect teens to? Scheduling the program for a consistent day and time allows teens to get into a pattern and to know that if they show up at the library on that day and time there will be something going on for them.

Provide the PR department with six months of calendar listings and write a description of the teen program that includes an invitation to come be part of a group—for teens to decide what's going to happen for the teens at the library and earn volunteer service hours. Because every program listing essentially recruits teens to join in on the planning, the message shifts to the important focus on teens as decision-makers and implementers of programming for themselves and their peers, and away from the clever program ideas offered by adults.

6. All Teen Programming Is Centralized. You and the Teens at Your Branch Don't Get a Choice of What Programs Are Available for Teens.

Library systems that try to apply the centralized programming model for teens may find that teen programming is difficult to establish and maintain. This failure of the centralized planning form can be wrongly interpreted as teens not wanting teen programming.

Centralized program planning treats all teens the same, although teens from different neighborhoods within a city may have vastly different needs and interests.

This is not story time.

Although I will advocate for libraries to have centralized programming assets available for use by teen services staff—it's a smart way to use resources across a system—be aware that the programs-in-a-box method has flaws. Programming developed centrally without teen involvement can be inflexible and unresponsive to their spontaneous, evolving interests. Because teens are detached from the development and implementation of the activities, they are bound to have interests that are not validated by centralized programming.

But even in a system with "programs in a box," there is an opportunity to begin low-level decision-making with teens (as described in chapter 2). If at the end of a teen program the question of what to do next week should be asked of the teens, present a menu of possible activities from which the teens can choose. Then they are at the very least making some basic decision about what activities they will engage in at the library. When the teens select, ask them if they will please come back and help you with the activity. You need their help. If this pattern is repeated, inevitably the teens will begin expressing ideas of their own. This helps you to communicate the particular service needs and interests of the community of teens you serve to the people who plan programming.

Presenters are a different story. If centralized programming means outside presenters are sporadically sent to your location (and I'm sure that unless the presenters are current celebrities or sports stars, attendance is rather sketchy), these should be scheduled in the same consistent manner as other teen programs, on the same day and time, that is, plug special programming into the regularly scheduled teen programming time slot.

7. You Get Angry about the Way Teens Are Treated at Your Library.

What's the old saying? You catch more flies with honey than vinegar. Diplomacy is important. What you don't want to do is alienate your coworkers. Remember that you are a professional, and that your actions and attitudes represent the teen services department. If the vibe is already negative, you only reinforce it with any displays of anger. Being angry isn't good for you—and it isn't good for teen services. This doesn't mean you turn a blind eye to what's going on in the organization; it means you keep things professional, and never take them personally. This also means sometimes you have to wait out negative people.

Look for opportunities to accentuate the positive aspects of teen services. Be vocal about how many hours teen volunteers have given the library over the last school year and how great the circulation numbers of YA fiction are. Make an effort to introduce teens to your crankiest coworkers. Once coworkers start to think of teens as individuals (and as human beings rather than a swarm of locusts) things might begin to get better.

Make an ally out of the local media—invite them to come to a teen program where your best and brightest teens are prepared to advocate for teen programming at the library. Look for outside partners like the PTA, local high school, or partner organizations. Have happy parents, or teens themselves, speak during library board meetings. If a manager hears how great teen services are, she might start to believe it and the dynamic might change. This kind of positive publicity can dramatically shift the attitude of staff toward teen services. Not to put too fine a point on it: if teen programming looks good, then your boss can look like a hero—a true humanitarian. That is pure honey.

8. Your Impulse Is to Give Teens Cash, Food, a Ride, a Place to Stay . . .

This is a good impulse, and will come naturally, particularly if you are an empathetic person. But know that going down this road probably violates an administrative directive or two that your library or municipality has put in place for a reason. There is just too much liability in this situation. Even if you think you are acting as a private citizen, opening the door of your car or home to a teen patron is a surefire way to get fired.

However, remember that you professionally connect people to information—and that is not just limited to books. If you know a teen in distress who needs a place to stay, this is the time to put to use your librarian superpowers and connect that teen to agencies in the community that can help. Do it right then and there in that moment of need (even if that means calling the police or child protective services).

Have I ever given a teen bus fare? Yes. Snuck a teen a Happy Meal? Yes. But I like to think I know where to draw the line between kindness and liability. Sometimes it is difficult not to feel helpless, but the way we can be of greatest service to a teen in crisis is to connect them with agencies that can help them in a sustainable way.

9. Teens Want to Say Hello by Hugging You.

Teens might not completely understand boundaries. They may want to hug you in the same way they would hug their friends. The goal here is to not make a big deal about this (while simultaneously not hugging, keeping your job, and not being creepy). This may sound like a joke, but it's not. It's a less-than-complicated maneuver. If a teen tries to hug you straight-on, quickly turn to the side so that you are standing next to them, arms down and hands-clasped in front of you (male librarian) or arms crossed in front of you (female librarian), and slightly incline your head sideways toward the teen. (The head thing is optional.)

Try this maneuver or simply laugh, and while taking a step back, say, "Please do not touch the librarian." This is guaranteed to get a laugh and to get your point across.

10. You Are Held Responsible for the Way Teens Act in the Library. If Someone Is Caught Doing Something Wrong You Find Yourself Chanting "Please Don't Let It Be a Teen."

I completely relate to this. For years, if someone was caught doing something wrong, I too found myself chanting, "Please don't let it be a teen." I think because teens are under additional scrutiny in the library, teen services librarians bear the burden of also being under increased scrutiny. After all, it is our mission to draw teens to the library, which is an outcome colleagues and security staff may not relish.

Years ago, I worked with a security guard who thought that no matter what went wrong—graffiti, knocked-over trash cans, book-drop violated—teens were to blame. I tried to appeal to the security guard's reason, and make a case that not all the teens who came to the library were "bad," not even the ones who had to be asked to leave. This got me nowhere. It was stressful, because I was taking on responsibility for the behavior of the teens. This security guard would always say to me, "Do you know what your kids did?" One day, I finally told him, "I don't have any kids—I don't know who you are talking about."

The ease with which teens are blamed for vandalism and defacing library property, coupled with my desire to advocate for teens, put me on the defensive. Adult services librarians are not held responsible for the behavior of adult patrons; children's librarians do not take responsibility for crying toddlers. Teen services librarians should not be held responsible for the behavior of teens—real or imaginary.

11. You Are Often Called to the Reference Desk to Help Teens—Whether You Are on Desk or Not. You Don't Really Mind Because You Worry That Teens Won't Be Treated Well.

This can be frustrating; it's not like teens speak a language only you can understand. But, this is also a moment when you can help your colleague to provide better service for teens *and* demonstrate how awesome you are with teens and what a great asset you are to the organization.

1. Tell your colleague, "I'm not really on desk right now—but I'd be glad to get things started." Tell your colleague to stay with you. Say "Stay with me." (Use command form, which gives her no other options.)
2. Make introductions to the teen: "Hi, I'm (your name) and this is (colleague's name)."
3. Facilitate the interview, asking the colleague for assistance. In this way the teen's request is essentially being satisfied by the colleague—with you acting as mediator (for both parties).
4. At some point while your colleague is watching, tell the teen, "You can always ask me or (colleague's name) if you need help finding anything." Smile. Go back to your desk feeling like a true team player.

5. Based on the professional development needs demonstrated by this transaction, devise a plan to ask your manager if you can conduct training on teen reference tactics for the entire branch staff.

STEPPING OUT OF THE WAY

Being a teen services librarian can be full of challenges, but it is a vocation filled with satisfaction and meaning. The clientele group is vibrant, eager, and will drive the library toward true innovation if we only step out of the way. This book encourages you to push the boundaries of teen participation, and asks you to apply a bit of teen services arithmetic by adding teens into every service equation. Ask where teens can fit into space planning and customization, program development and implementation, collection development, and even into the day-to-day operations that are the very fabric of the library.

Don't be confused by the notion of what a library is *supposed* to be. The library is always in the process of becoming. Trust your service instinct and your passion, and let them inform your actions.

At times, the challenges you experience might seem too great for the solutions found in books, but remember that you have allies.

The first is the "teen you." Shy, awkward, wild, confident, creative, brilliant: whatever you were like as a teen, let your younger self inform your service attitude. Let this guide you and give you the determination to abandon control as teens take charge of their library experience. This is not simply a responsiveness to teen library users' desires but a reliance upon their participation in the "process" that is the library.

Your second ally is the teen community you are tasked to serve. Trust these teens, and value their ideas, opinions, and abilities. They are your greatest allies and partners. After all, the teens are the *why* behind your job—not the books, not the authors, not the traditions of the past—but the young individuals standing in front of you today who rely on you to be their advocate and ally.

To provide dedicated teen services is to help crystallize the expectations that teens will have of their library for life. It is an opportunity for the library to harness and apply their energy and ideas. Teen services can lead the library on its way to authentically becoming an institution where the community gains and creates knowledge and meaning together as a shared experience: The Participatory Library for everyone.

INDEX

A

abuse, 94–95
accessibility, 82–85, 92–93
adult services, transition to, 22–23
adults
    attitudes of, 30–31
    teens-only space and, 17–18
    See also parents
advocacy, 108
affinity space, 7–9
Albrecht, Steven, 79
allegiances, building, 63
American Library Association,
    82–83, 92
analog display wall, 7
architects, 24
artwork
    display of, 7
    performance space and, 13
attitudes
    adult, 30–31
    librarian, 57

B

behavior
    guidelines for, 70, 71–72, 84–85.
        See also codes of conduct
    managing problems, 72–80
    responsibility for, 109–110
Bernier, Anthony, 2, 3, 20
book clubs, 46
Boston Public Library, 43
Bryant, Sheila, 86
Buckley, Don, 14–15
burnout, 102
Burton Barr Library (Phoenix), 16

C

Carnegie, Andrew, 4
Carnegie Model, 4–5
centralized programming development,
    43–44, 107
Cerritos Library (California), 14–15
Chicago Public Library, 22, 43
child protection policies, 89
children
    older, 17, 19–20, 21, 41–43
    youth services and, 64
codes of conduct, 69–72. *See also*
    behavior
colleagues
    communication with, 61, 108
    modeling service strategies for,
        61–62, 110–111
    training and, 63
    See also staff
Committee on Public Libraries in
    the Knowledge Society
    (Denmark), 10
common ground, finding, 97–99
communication
    with colleagues, 61, 108
    of rules, 71–72
    with teens, 103–104
community services, 93–94, 109
confidentiality, 89, 93–96. *See also*
    privacy
*Confronting the Challenges of
    Participatory Culture* (Jenkins
    et al.), 6
consistency, 74–76, 106
creation library, 13
curfews, 88–89

D

daytime curfews, 88–89
demographics, 32
discrimination, 21–22, 30, 83
diversity, 97–99

E

Enoch Pratt Free Library (Baltimore), 87
expectations, 1–2, 37–38
experience economy, 14

F

first contacts, 59–60
form, function and, 3–4, 15
four-space model, 9–16, 9*fig*
"Free Access to Libraries for Minors"
    (ALA), 92
"Freedom to Read" (ALA), 83
"Freedom to View" (ALA), 83
Friends of the Library groups, 34–35
funding, 34–35

G

Garza, Violeta, 97–99
"Geography of No!," 3
Givens, Cherie, 94
guerilla/stealth programming, 50–51

H

Houston Public Library, 84
hugging, 109
Hymowitz, Kay S., 41

I

image, crafting positive, 61
in loco parentis, doctrine of, 85–86, 94
inspiration space, 9*fig*, 14–16
interests, space and, 8–9

J

Jenkins, Henry, 6
Jones, Patrick, 71

K

Kitchen, Carrie, 100–102

L

large-scale one-off programming,
    51–52
large-scale participation, 47–48
layout of library, 33–34

learning, forms of, 11
learning space, 9*fig*, 10–11
librarian
    expectations of, 37–38
    role of, 35–36, 55–56
    self-perception of, 35–36
    solo, 100–102
    See also colleagues; staff
library anxiety, 56
"Library Bill of Rights," 82–83
limitations. *See* restrictions on use
listening skills, 103–105
location of library, 32–33

M

make-and-leave programming, 51
make-and-take programming, 51
makerspaces/maker culture, 8, 13–14
meeting space, 9*fig*, 11–13
Mellon, Constance, 56

N

networking, 100–101
Nordic Library of the Future, 9–16, 9*fig*

O

open access, 82–85
orientations, 21, 22
outreach, 32–33

P

paging, 89–91
parents
    accompaniment by, 21
    advocacy and, 39
    communication and, 66
    family rules and, 92–93
    notification of, 79
    of older children, 19, 41–42, 43, 64
    privacy and, 89
    requests from, 90–91
    space dynamics and, 17
    See also adults; in loco parentis,
        doctrine of
participation, small-scale to large-scale,
    47–48
participatory culture theory, 6–7
performance space, 9*fig*, 13–14
police involvement, 79
privacy
    day-to-day situations and, 81–82

possible infringements of, 83, 89–93
real-world tactics for, 93–96
violations of, 87
programming
    barriers to, 29–38
    centralized, 43–44, 107
    challenges regarding, 41–49,
        106–107
    consistency of, 49, 52
    development of, 48
    forms of, 49–52
    guerilla/stealth, 50–51
    past failures of, 31–32
    planning, 38–41
    promotion of, 53
    rationale for, 28–29
    real-world tactics for, 49–54
    scheduling, 49, 52, 53–54
    service context for, 27
    space for, 33–34
    teen input and, 36, 37, 38, 39–40
public address system, 89–91

R
readers' advisory tips, 65–67
registration requirements, 21
relationships, building, 63
resources, limited, 101
restrictions on use, 21–22, 69–70,
    84–85, 87–89
returns from suspensions, 77–79
rules
    communicating, 71–72
    consistency and, 74–76
    separate, for teens, 69–70

S
San José Public Library, 90
Schenectady Public Library (New
    York), 85
school libraries, 94
schools, 32–33. *See also* truancy
self-perception of librarians, 35–36
sensitive situations, assistance with,
    93–94
service dynamics
    barriers and, 58–60
    crafting, 55–56
    different styles and, 57
    real-world tactics for, 65–67
service points, 57–60

service strategies, modeling, 61–63
Shoemaker, Joel, 71
signs, 71–72
small-scale participation, 47–48
small-scale recurring programming, 51
space
    challenges regarding, 19–22
    dedicated, 1–2
    development of, 5–7
    form and function of, 3–5
    getting started, 23–24
    inspiration, 9*fig*, 14–16
    interests and, 8–9
    learning, 9*fig*, 10–11
    meaning of, 2–3
    meeting, 9*fig*, 11–13
    models of, 7–16
    performance, 9*fig*, 13–14
    programming in, 33–34
    real-world tactics for, 23–24
    teen participation and, 5–7
    teens-only, 16–18
spontaneous/impromptu
        programming, 50
staff
    dedicated teen services, 64–65
    effectiveness of, 60–63
    importance of, 20–21
    training for, 101, 111
    See also colleagues; librarians;
        volunteers
status offenses, 85–86
stealth/guerilla programming, 50–51
Suellentrop, Tricia, 36
Sullivan, Louis, 3–4
suspensions, 77–79

T
Takahashi, Deborah, 103–105
teen advisory groups, 40
teen leadership groups, 41, 48
Teen Space Guidelines (YALSA), 5
third space, 12
time of day restrictions, 86–89
Toledo-Lucas County Public Library
    (Ohio), 87–88
training, 63, 101, 111
transition to adult services,
    22–23
truancy, 85–86, 87–88, 95
tweens, 17, 19–20, 21, 41–43

V

visibility, 12–13
volunteers, 22, 40, 62–63, 88, 99,
106, 108

W

Wilmington Memorial Library
(Massachusetts), 43
Winfield (Illinois) Public Library, 87

Y

Young Adult Library Services
Association (YALSA),
5, 16–17, 40
youth services, 64
youth development models, 29

CPSIA information can be obtained
at www.ICGtesting.com
Printed in the USA
BVHW031659220822
645209BV00023B/440

9 780838 913420